BRICKMAN'S BIG BOOK OF BETTER BUILDS

RYAN McNAUGHT

LEGO Certified Professional

For Tracy, Riley
and Alex.

BRICKMAN'S BIG BOOK OF BETTER BUILDS

RYAN McNAUGHT

murdoch books

Sydney | London

CONTENTS

SKILL ONE
DESIGN AND PREPARE 12

SKILL TWO
FORM AND STRUCTURE 42

SKILL THREE
SCALE AND SHAPE 76

SKILL FOUR
SNOT 110

SKILL FIVE

TELLING
A STORY 140

SKILL SIX

DETAILS 176

SKILL SEVEN

THE NEXT
LEVEL 228

WELCOME

Hello, I'm Ryan, but everyone knows me as 'Brickman'. I'm a LEGO® certified professional, one of only 22 in the world and the only one in the Southern Hemisphere. It's my job to make cool and incredible LEGO models for museums, stores and events around the world. I am also the judge on *LEGO Masters Australia*. Along with Hamish Blake, I get to watch the contestants on the show perform all manner of cool LEGO trickery, culminating in the most amazing and creative LEGO models.

During the filming of the third season of the show, I was talking with Hamish and the executive producer, David McDonald (an award-winning modelmaker in his own right), and we were asking, 'What is the secret to making the best model? What's the recipe for success?' We couldn't pin it down to one simple thing, because each build involves overcoming different specific challenges, whether that be in terms of structure, storytelling or style.

My experience from well over a decade of professional LEGO building, along with coaching the *LEGO Masters* contestants to get the most out of their boundless creativity, has made me realise that each successful build involves a series of key skills. Knowing what these are and how to apply them can open up a whole new world of possibilities in your model-making. This book was devised to guide you through these skills: answer your questions, solve any problems and give you a solid foundation for your creative process.

This book is different to my previous ones: it's a bit more technical, at times showing you some pretty advanced LEGO skills. It walks you through the creative process of LEGO builds from design to completion, filling in the nitty-gritty of everything you need to know to make amazing models – all of the things that will help you on your way to one day taking my job!

I can't pretend to know every LEGO element and every way they can be connected to each other, but I see LEGO building as a continuously evolving thing. Not only does The LEGO Group itself come up with new parts and colours every year, but builders all over the world, just like you, constantly come up with new ways to connect and use existing LEGO elements.

My hope for you is that no matter what kind of LEGO builder you are, you'll read this book and learn at least one new technique or concept, and you'll use your new-found skills to make your LEGO models even more fun and innovative. I'd love to see what you create; share your builds on social media using the hashtag #brickmansbetterbuilds.

Go forth and make the incredible!

RYAN McNAUGHT
LEGO® CERTIFIED PROFESSIONAL

HOW TO USE THIS BOOK

This book walks you through how to approach a LEGO® build from start to finish. Each chapter covers a key set of skills, and these skills are built on as you progress. I recommend that you read the book through once, then dip in and out of various sections as needed, to use as a reference guide whilst tackling a build.

In these pages I cover some in-depth processes that you need to understand about your LEGO models. As with all LEGO things, there is no right or wrong: it's not a Boolean equation to solve a problem. The LEGO System is a 'system of play'.

A 'SYSTEM OF PLAY'? HOW DOES THAT WORK?

SYSTEM
an assemblage or combination of things or parts forming a complex or unitary whole

PLAY
exercise or action by way of amusement or recreation

Definitions from *Macquarie Dictionary Online*, 2022, Macquarie Dictionary Publishers, an imprint of Pan Macmillan Australia Pty Ltd, macquariedictionary.com.au

Fancy making something that combines those two things! Well played, Danish gurus at LEGO HQ, well played indeed.

The LEGO System, though it has many thousands of parts and squillions of possible combinations, does have constraints; lots of constraints – and that's why your mind boggles when you see an incredible LEGO creation: the sheer fact that someone has managed to work through all the problems and found all the answers to make something incredible. But it's all part of the play: you can make ANYTHING out of LEGO parts, you have ZERO constraints; creativity is limitless and endless. A 'system of play' combines two polar opposites: constraints and infinite freedom.

That's why I love LEGO bricks so much.

Hi! I'm Brickman, and you'll find me wandering through the pages of this book with pro tips and advice on how to get the most out of your LEGO System. Try the Brickman Challenge and count how many times you spot me in the pages... and see if you can find any impostors.

WHAT LEGO BRICKS DO I NEED?

The great thing about this book is that you don't
need a particular LEGO set or specific bricks; LEGO
bricks are so versatile they can literally be anything.
A single 2x4 LEGO brick can be part of a plane, a tree,
a tiger or even a LEGO sandwich.

This book won't show you exactly how to build
a specific model – it isn't like a set of LEGO instructions
on how to make something. Instead it will teach you
the underlying principles of what makes a LEGO
model stand out.

Along the way I'll refer to certain LEGO parts;
however, it's not a problem if you don't have a specific
part, as you can solve the same challenge in many
different ways. The only thing you need to get the
most out of the parts you have is your imagination.
Remember, it's not about how many LEGO bricks you
have, but how you use them. There's no right or wrong.

If you see any LEGO language that's unfamiliar,
you can look it up in the Glossary on page 294.

As you go about building your own creations,
it's important to remember that you won't always
get it right straight away; I certainly don't. Some
of the ideas and techniques in this book take time
to learn and master, and *it's always okay to make
mistakes*. While mistakes might be frustrating,
one of the reasons the LEGO System is so great
is that you can take it apart and try again. And if
you discover a better way to do something than
the way I've described in this book, that's fantastic!

A NOTE FOR LEGO EXPERTS

There'll be things in here that you already know.
In fact, some of them will be second nature to you,
so much so that you won't even think about the
process that you are employing. If that's the case,
you're in great shape, but you can still use the skills
and techniques in this book to keep pushing the
limits of your building practice. Whether it's
developing new or better techniques, challenging
yourself to build bigger (or smaller) models, or finding
different ways to tell a story, there are always new
challenges to discover with LEGO bricks.

BRICKMAN'S CASTLE BUILD

Castles are LEGO model staples as they offer plenty of opportunities for creativity: a bit of fantasy, a bit of history and a lot of fun. You can include as many different features as you can think of, from a princess at the top of a tower to a dragon in the dungeon. You can make battles and feasts and flags and crowns; the possibilities are endless.

To illustrate and unify all the concepts covered here, I've created the ultimate castle model as a case study that uses all of the skills and techniques you'll learn in this book. Look for the yellow **BRICKMAN'S CASTLE BUILD** pages at the end of each chapter to see the theory put into practice. Words in bold indicate how I've used the skills you've just been reading about to create the epic castle model.

Here you'll find drawings and concepts of the model, close-ups of tricky techniques and behind-the-bricks photos of the project as it's being built. If it helps you learn, you can try replicating the project from this book as you read; however, the intention is to show just one way the skills and knowledge in the book can come together to create an impressive LEGO build.

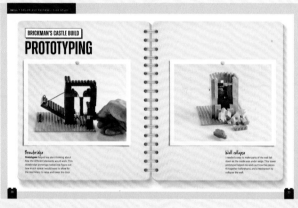

DESIGN AND PREPARE

1

PREPARATION can make all the difference between a mediocre model and a stunning showpiece. As well as questions of **DESIGN** and **STYLE**, there might be logistical and brick inventory concerns. **PLANNING** can be the difference between the **SUCCESS** or failure of a project: it's like eating your vegetables before you have dessert. Get the serious bit out of the way so you can enjoy the fun stuff.

DESIGN

Before you start building any LEGO® project – even for the simplest models, but especially for a large build – you need to prepare. Designing your model before you start building is a chance for you to refine your idea and improve it to make it the best version it can be. There may be sections you want to include in your build that you need to take into consideration before the rest of the model is built, or the inclusions won't fit. Or worse, you might get towards the end of the build and find you've run out of parts. Projects that are not designed and prepared properly can end up looking odd or malformed. Having a good design and a well-thought-out plan will ensure you can include everything you wish in a pleasing, sturdy and well-structured model.

It might sound as though planning every single detail will suck all the fun out of building, but think of it as a way to include everything you want, and ensure that your crazy ideas succeed and don't just fall into a heap. You'll still have fun building, but it's more likely you'll end up with an amazing and presentable model at the end.

Building LEGO models from sets can help inspire you. Seeing how others have solved problems and figuring out how LEGO models are planned and built can help you tackle your own building problems. You can learn new techniques and new combinations of parts to achieve interesting constructions and try out new ideas.

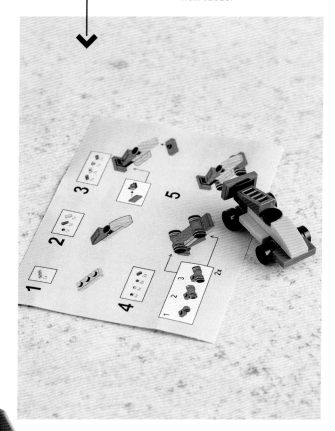

Stop! Put down those bricks. No, seriously, put them down. Before you jump headlong into creating the next masterpiece, let's take a moment to consider what you're about to do.

INSPIRATION

Inspiration can come from anywhere, so collect images and stories of things you find interesting or amazing. Gather samples of materials that your subject might be made from. Making a scrapbook of bits and pieces – either physically or digitally – will be a great resource for you to look over when you are feeling uninspired. Join an online community, such as a LEGO builders' forum. Looking at what has been made by others can help you get ideas and inspiration for your own work. Watch or read interviews and features on builders (even if you're not into the subject of their build) to see how they approached building, achieved interesting features and solved problems. Start an Instagram account to follow lots of different accounts and hashtags that fire your imagination, not just the LEGO Group and other LEGO builders but any subject you like: art, design, illustration, books, street art, sports, pop culture, performance, music, dance, animation, movies, video games, space exploration, vehicles, technology, astronomy, fairytales, fantasy, mysticism, religion, plants, animals, superheroes, ceramic frogs or absolutely anything that inspires you.

Making a LEGO 'doodle' is quite similar to doodling with a pencil and paper. Browse through your LEGO parts and pick out some pieces. It doesn't matter whether they're standard bricks or special pieces you like the look of. Try putting them together in different ways. Pick out some interesting colours and try them next to each other. Grab a handful of pieces in your chosen colours and build something. There are no rules here, just pick up some parts and go for it.

Sometimes an idea will come to you without even trying. Letting your mind whirr away over different things will help to oil the cogs of your imagination. Your idea may be weird and alien, even a bit silly, but that's no reason not to give it a chance. Sometimes the strangest ideas turn out to be the best.

Try building something, such as a flower, with different pieces until you achieve the effect you want.

Maybe you want to mash different things you like together to make something new. If you like horses, plants and the colour blue, you could have fun building a combination of those.

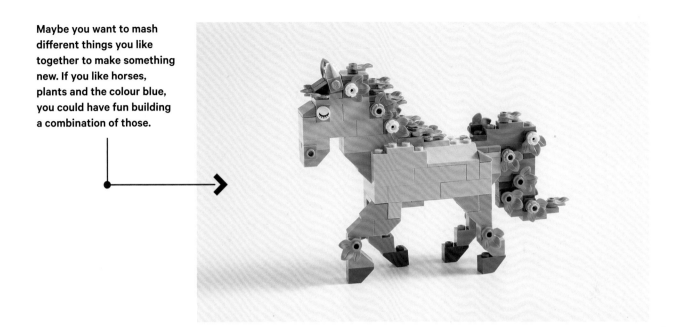

FIND YOUR PASSION

When deciding what to build, it's good to start with things you enjoy. Doing a bit of exploration of what's close to your heart can lead to many different places. If you've been building with the LEGO System for a while, it's probably a good idea to think about the kinds of things that you enjoy building and consider expanding that subject: spaceships, buildings, robots, characters, monsters, towns, vehicles, cupcakes or whatever you like. There is no right or wrong.

If you have a particular hobby or interest, it might be worth looking deeper into that subject. What fills your heart with joy? These are the things that drive us, that inspire us and are perfect subjects for making models. There is no problem with making the same subject over and over, improving and refining it each time and coming up with new ways to represent the things you are building. Try building with different pieces, different colours or even a different type of thing. If you like flowers, how is building a rose different from a dandelion? Finding what you love may take time, but there's no rush and no rules for this. The great thing about the LEGO System is that you can build whatever you like.

A change of scenery is good for firing the brain cells, so go for a walk and let your mind wander. Go somewhere new: an unfamiliar place might spark new thoughts or new ways of doing the same old things.

RESEARCH

To prepare for a build, it's always a good idea to get to know your subject. If you know as much as you can about the thing you're going to build, it'll help you create a better version of the model. You'll be able to include more detail and 'insider knowledge' to make it more realistic, accurate and believable for the viewer. Expand your knowledge of the subject by looking at resources such as books, videos, websites and more. Try to find out enough about the subject to answer as many questions as you can, such as:

» What are the dimensions? How tall, wide, long and deep is the thing?
» What colours are involved? What's it made of?
» Where is it? When did it exist?
» What is its history? Where does its name come from?
» What did it do?

Research any other particularly relevant details about your subject that you feel are essential to the build.

BRAINSTORMING

Once you know a lot about your subject it will be easier for you to brainstorm the build. You don't need to make things up if you know the subject inside out.

You may wonder what the point is of brainstorming a model if the subject is quite straightforward. But brainstorming is not only great for building – it can also give you ideas for displaying a model. Maybe with a bit of brainstorming you can come up with a unique way of presenting your model that is eye-catching and different.

Gather your research together and look for things of interest. Write down a list of words associated with the subject and make links or connections between them to try to spark some ideas.

Write down all the ideas you have come up with, and from that make a list of the things that you want to include in your build. Making a list like this means you won't forget anything important while you're designing and building the model, and ensures that all of your cool little ideas get included.

Brainstorming should help you to individualise the build and make it uniquely yours.

If your first reaction is, 'Oh no, that's too hard to make', just put that idea aside before abandoning it outright, because you may be surprised what you can achieve.

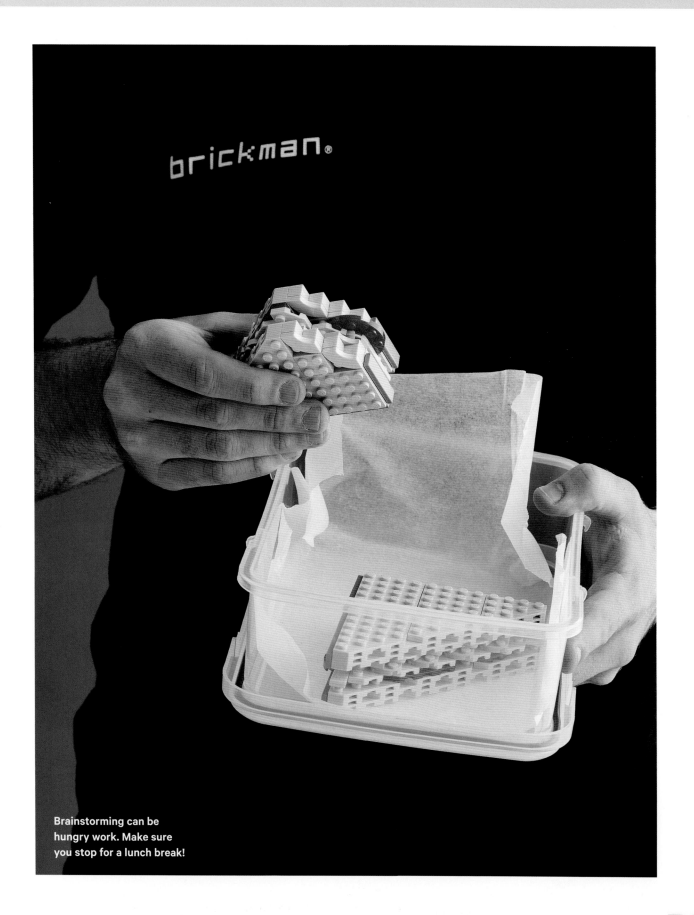

Brainstorming can be hungry work. Make sure you stop for a lunch break!

Sketch out your idea on paper (or using a tablet if you are comfortable with drawing that way) and include as many details as you can. Don't worry if it's not a work of art.

THINKING IN 3D

Now that you know what you want to make and what needs to be included, it's time to sketch out your subject with pencil and paper. This is just to get your ideas down, so don't be too precious about it; it doesn't have to be a work of art, and you can change it as much as you like. It's just a really quick way to translate your abstract ideas into two dimensions, before you take it one step further into 3D.

Sketch out what you think the overall model should look like. Make it as simple as you like. Represent the elements of your build as simple shapes and lines. You can erase the shapes and rearrange them as much as you like. If your sketch has become too messy, just start again. Try different positions and arrangements to see what will work best to display all the features you wish to include.

It can be helpful to divide your drawing up into basic shapes such as circles and triangles (see *Shape*, pages 84–85).

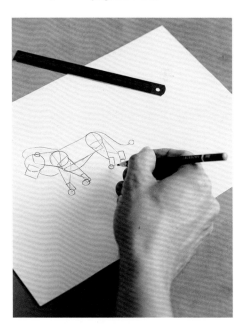

MAKE AN ORTHOGONAL SKETCH

Once you have a few sketches and a bit of an idea of the placement of everything in your model, you should do more of a detailed plan. This sketch will be more precise and will look at the model from different angles – usually the front, top, sides and back. Make sure that the different views of your plan drawings are at the same scale: the front and side views should be the same height; the front and top views should be the same width.

Start with a side view, as in the sketch of the lion, for example, and align the different views on the paper when you draw them so that you can easily compare them. This is called an 'orthogonal sketch'. Drawing the model from different perspectives will

force you to consider how it will fit together in 3D. Any element that exists in one 'view' of this drawing should have a corresponding version of itself in the other views. Each element should be present in every view: top, bottom, left and right. Some of the elements may be 'behind' others, so draw these in with dotted lines to represent how they would appear if you could see them through the other parts.

It can be easier to see where elements might be and how big they are in the different views of your drawing by ruling in horizontal and vertical guidelines, as shown in the finished drawing on page 23. These lines can help you to ensure that the objects are the same in all of your different views.

To get a better idea of how the parts of your model might go together you can redraw your orthogonal sketch larger and with more detail (grid paper will make this easier). Take your time with this and start out with the basic outline, lightly drawn. It's okay to make positioning changes if you need to: this is still the planning stage. You don't even need to be thinking of it as a LEGO model just yet, as that may restrict your imagination. But by this stage you should have a much clearer idea of what the model will look like in 3D and how the different elements might interact and connect.

Spend more time drawing parts of the model that are detailed and important. Use your eraser to make sure you get this correct, and do it in all views. Add more detail and darkness to the drawing, erasing any lines or guides so you can see the model more clearly and ensure that it will be able to exist in 3D in the way you have envisioned it.

At this point you should consider how you want your model to exist in the real world: its width, height, depth, length, detail, texture and colour, as well as having a good idea of how it will connect together. If you are still unsure about any part of this you can continue drawing or even make a simple prototype (see *Prototyping,* page 32), but make sure you are well acquainted with your build and have a clear idea of it in your mind before you begin building. You don't want to get midway through the build to find that something can't work the way you thought it would and have to return to the planning stage. Fix your mistakes in the planning stage before you have wasted hours building those mistakes.

From these final drawings you can start to look at your plan and think about it as LEGO parts. The shapes that make up the model now need to be thought of as segments to be built (see **Skill 3: Scale and Shape** for more).

**Start thinking about the LEGO parts
you will use to create the build.**

STYLE

The secret to creating professional-looking models is making sure that the build is consistent in style. If you make models with no particular style in mind, you can end up with a mishmash of decorations and techniques that look messy and random. Styles can be defined by their use of two key elements: shape and line. For example, arches and circles are the dominant shapes in an art deco style, while straight lines and squares are more modernist features.

The small and large circles in this textured piece are reminiscent of art deco style.

Consider building your model in an original style, different from what has been done before. Different styles may evoke emotions, fire your imagination, and inspire you to add unique touches to your builds. There are many styles you can choose from, such as:

» realistic	» mini-land
» cartoon	» steampunk
» abstract	» futuristic
» chibi (cute anime)	» anime
» blocky	» art deco
» caricature	» impressionist.

Depending on the features of the style, there may be pros and cons to building in that manner, which would be different for every model. But choosing an interesting and original style can make the difference between your model being a standout or just run of the mill. It may be a matter of finding the ways to build certain features to really nail the look you are going for. Be creative: try to represent the style as faithfully as you can.

Once you have decided on the style, you have to replicate it with LEGO parts. To achieve a certain style, you should represent its major features, so look at the kinds of line, shape, form, colour and texture that are present in the style and decide how you will represent these.

All styles can be defined by their use of two key elements: shape and line.

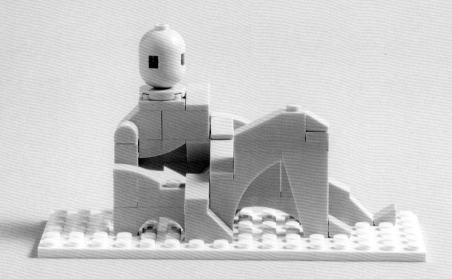

**Modernist: after sculptor
Henry Moore.**

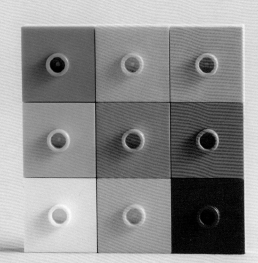

**Blocky style with
cute colours.**

This complicated
machine has repeated
details that take up lots
of LEGO parts, space
and time.

SELECTIVE COMPRESSION

Selective compression is a technique of picking out features and details that really define your style or subject, and making them the most important things in the build. Enlarge key features a little to emphasise them, and reduce or omit less important things. Much like a caricature, you exaggerate the recognisable parts, capturing the essence of the subject.

You can also reduce the numbers of a repeated feature so that it feels like the original, but isn't as crowded, as in the examples left and below. The smaller machine still tells the same story as the larger one, without the need for too many intricate details and extra LEGO parts.

A caricature of Jeff Goldblum shows selective compression.

Selective compression shows the same machine as at left, with fewer parts but still showing the essential workings.

27

SCOPING THE PROJECT

Planning, planning and more planning. Take stock of your LEGO supplies and make sure you have everything you need to complete the model. Where will you construct the model, and do you have a large enough space to make the whole thing in one piece, or will you need to make it in smaller modules that can be put together later? How much time do you have to build it? If your time is limited, what parts of the build will be priorities?

TAKING STOCK

Before starting the project, you should take stock of everything you will need to complete it. Knowing what you have to work with or what extra things you might need can help you to smoothly complete the project the way you have envisioned it.

WHAT PARTS AND COLOURS DO YOU HAVE?

If you need multiples of particular parts then this will be of concern if you don't have the required amount. You may need to alter your plans. Maybe you have other parts in the same or a similar colour that you could use in a creative way, or you could try an alternative technique (such as *Selective compression*, page 27).

DO YOU HAVE ENOUGH LEGO PARTS?

This can be important not only for the size of your model but also whether the model is achievable right now. If the model is needed immediately, you won't have time to get any extra supplies, so taking stock of what you already have will help to evaluate this. If the model isn't so urgent, taking stock can help you to see what you already have, so you won't need to acquire extra, unnecessary parts.

FINDING SUPPLIES

If your LEGO collection is not up to the task of making the model, there are several ways to get the pieces you want, each with pros and cons.

- » You can buy LEGO sets that include the pieces you want. This is the way most people tend to acquire LEGO parts, but if you need a lot of specific pieces, it can get pricey.
- » You can buy specific pieces from LEGO.com. The LEGO website has a 'pick-a-brick' section, which has a specific selection of currently produced parts, but perhaps not absolutely everything that you may need.
- » If you have a LEGO store near you, they may have a 'pick-a-brick' wall that allows you to fill a fixed-price container with whatever pieces they have in stock, although they may not have everything you need.

- » You can buy LEGO parts from online resellers, such as Bricklink or Brick Owl. You can select the parts you want and order them from many different sellers all over the world; the only drawback here is that you might have to pay a lot for the pieces and the postage from far-off lands, so be careful of your budget.
- » People quite often sell LEGO sets and parts online in social media selling groups, or at garage sales, or even charity shops. You may even find older LEGO sets on sale at large department stores. It pays to look around.

BUILDING SPACE

Usually if you are building something large you should be building it in a large space; however, sometimes this is not possible, so you need to make the most of the space you do have. Even with a smaller available space you can make larger models by building them in sections that can fit together. Making your large models modular means you can build them as pieces in a smaller space and put the pieces together elsewhere.

A good space for LEGO building will have a workbench or table where you can spread out containers and work on your model. It would be ideal if the table was in the centre of the room so that you can move around it and work on the model from all sides. If your LEGO storage space is nearby, so much the better: it will save you carrying boxes of bricks and LEGO parts.

BUILDING TIME

Estimating how long things will take is a good idea. Don't be afraid to re-evaluate the time needed once you've finished a section of the build; if it took more or less time than you thought you can adjust the whole project length. After you've made a few smaller practice projects you can apply that experience to larger ones.

If you have a project plan you can set targets and milestones to help you manage your time effectively. Prioritising the most important elements of the build will help keep you motivated to complete the model in the allotted time. Write a list of the elements in order of importance, and you can start at the top and work your way down the list. If you are held up in one section, leave that and go on with a different section so that you don't waste time.

Your LEGO toolkit can even be contained in a LEGO toolbox!

PRIORITIES

In what order do things need to be done? When you consider building your model you may need to tackle things in a certain order. Usually, all the details and the finishing touches are done at the end, but if you are designing a building, for example, the interior details will need to be completed before you can put on the windows and outer walls, so that needs to be part of the consideration of the order of things.

TOOLKIT

You may find certain tools useful when working with LEGO parts. A rubber-tipped mallet is handy to make sure your brickwork is pushed all the way down: tiny gaps can add up to big, ugly cracks in your model and pieces being misaligned. This can cause stability issues so take it from me: use the mallet. A brick separator will help to save your fingers if you have to pull up bricks. Tweezers are good for placing small pieces in tight places and applying stickers. Brushes and paper towel are good for cleaning LEGO parts, as is a rubber air-puffer bulb for dust and particles. A small ruler can help keep things aligned. This is just a general list and you may have other needs, depending on the model, that you must consider and find solutions for.

PROTOTYPING

When you are preparing to make a model, you may have planned to use a new technique for a particular part of it, or perhaps it's just a shape or size you are unsure of. The planning stage is a great time to prototype that part to make sure it'll work the way you'd hoped. To make a prototype, build the part in its simplest form, concentrating on size and shape rather than colours and details.

When you prototype important details you can be prepared for how to integrate them into the model. Once you know the size or shape of the prototype, you can build an appropriate place and connection in the model to hold this piece. If you hadn't prototyped the section, you might have made it all the way to the end of the build and then realised that you had no way of including it.

Make the prototype the same size as it will be in the finished model, to help you visualise the details. You can also make prototypes of any pieces with moving parts or actions, so that you can see how much space the mechanism takes up and where you need to incorporate it into your build.

MAQUETTE

If you are making a very complex model, such as something in human form, another kind of prototype you can make is a small, simplified version of the model, made from modelling clay or other materials you like to work with, such as wax or plaster. This is called a 'maquette', which is French for – you guessed it – 'small model'. Maquettes can help you to visualise how the 3D forms of your model will connect and interact, allowing you to strengthen it, balance it and rearrange any elements you need to.

It doesn't need to be a perfect work of art: think of it as a 3D sketch. It can help you to see when your model needs some kind of support for sections that are flimsy without special internal structure. It can also help you to see if the pose or action you intend for your model looks awkward or unnatural. It always helps to see your design in 3D so you can iron out any problems you might encounter when building the actual model.

When you're building prototypes, don't worry about the colours of the LEGO parts. Get the shapes and connections working first.

Use any material you like
to build a maquette of your
model. Modelling clay is
a good choice.

33

DIGITAL BUILDING

Another great way of designing a model is by using LEGO software and building models on your computer. Digital building has the advantage of having an unlimited supply of LEGO parts, so you can build as large or as small as you like. You can also export images or instructions from the programs once you have completed a digital build.

DEDICATED SOFTWARE

There are some excellent software programs that you can use to design awesome models.

The LEGO Group has free software of its own called 'LEGO Digital Designer' or 'LDD'. It is available for Mac and PC platforms and it makes it quite easy to construct projects from a wide selection of parts. You can also render simple images and building instructions with it. There is a lot of online

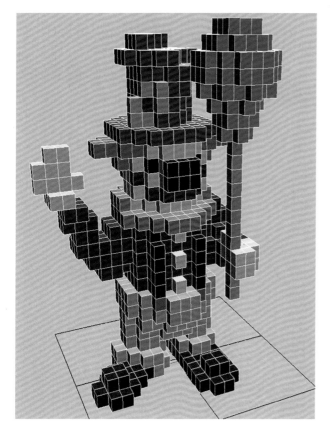

documentation, plus YouTube tutorials and social media communities that can help you to get started and develop your building skills in this program. Unfortunately, the LEGO Group is no longer supporting the program, so the parts you want may not be available; plus the software includes pieces in colours that aren't actually available in sets or online.

Another useful software program, which is now endorsed by the LEGO Group, is Bricklink's Studio. Available for Mac and PC from the Bricklink website, this is a fully featured piece of software that includes integration with Bricklink's online shop if you wish to buy pieces in that way. The building is a little harder in this program and it takes longer to get going on making models, but it's more precise, and the rendering looks quite realistic if you want to make images. It is updated frequently and has a large range of pieces in many colours. It will also indicate when you use a piece that is not available in the real world, making it easier to choose pieces for your model when building it for real. With some effort you can make detailed and nice-looking instructions, see an average price for the pieces you are using and make shopping lists of required pieces.

OTHER USEFUL PROGRAMS

There is other software that you can use to do different things, such as import 3D model files and have them converted to bricks, or import a picture and have it transferred into a brick mosaic. There are all kinds of programs for digital prototypes that you might need to make your models, so do your research to find which ones you prefer.

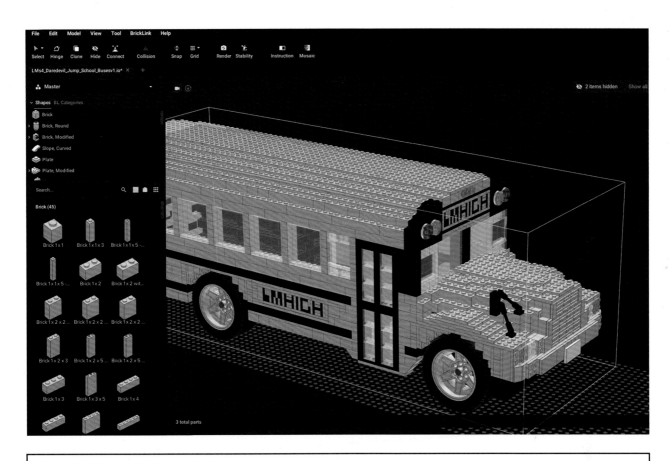

One of the downsides to planning models digitally is that the size is unrestrained and the build can get very big, very quickly. Larger models cost more, so sometimes your digital creation is too expensive to actually build in real life. Digital models aren't affected by weight restraints or gravity and can be unbalanced or have weak connections. In addition, it's more time-consuming to reconfigure and change digital models, whereas real models can be broken apart and sections can be easily swapped out.

BRICKMAN'S CASTLE BUILD
PLANNING

Early design sketches were a great way to get all of the brainstorming down on paper.

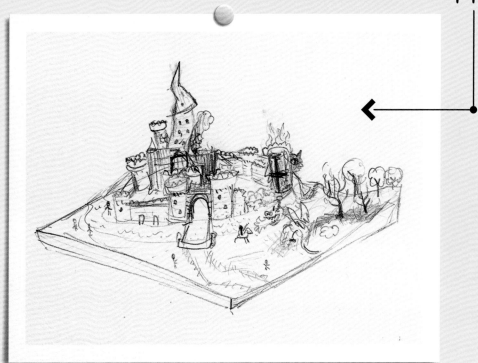

Inspiration for this castle build was not difficult to come by: just about everyone has a favourite fairytale or historic castle that gets their imagination working and ignites their **passion**. And it's always a pleasure to do **research** on a favourite topic. After a little **brainstorming** with the Brickman team, I decided on a few things that were essential for my castle: walls, towers and interior buildings, a keep, a king and queen, a princess, a dragon, a heroic figure, a jester, a wizard, a magical mishap, a wonky wizard's tower, a battle, a moat with a drawbridge, a catapult, cobblestones, horses and knights. With that list, I went about **sketching** a castle model.

I decided to use a cartoonish, not completely realistic **style**, to keep the build detail to a minimum.

Orthogonal drawings of the castle and some of the smaller parts were important stages in the planning process.

Bricklink's Studio **software** enabled me to digitally construct the castle and start **scoping out** the project in terms of **time**, **space** and the **tools** and LEGO **parts** I'll need to bring it to life.

BRICKMAN'S CASTLE BUILD

PROTOTYPING

Drawbridge

Prototypes helped me start thinking about how the different elements would work. This drawbridge prototype helped me figure out how much space I would need to allow for the machinery to raise and lower the door.

Wall collapse

I needed a way to make parts of the wall fall down as the castle was under seige. This tower prototype helped me work out how the pieces fit together beforehand, and a mechanism to collapse the wall.

BRICKMAN'S CASTLE BUILD

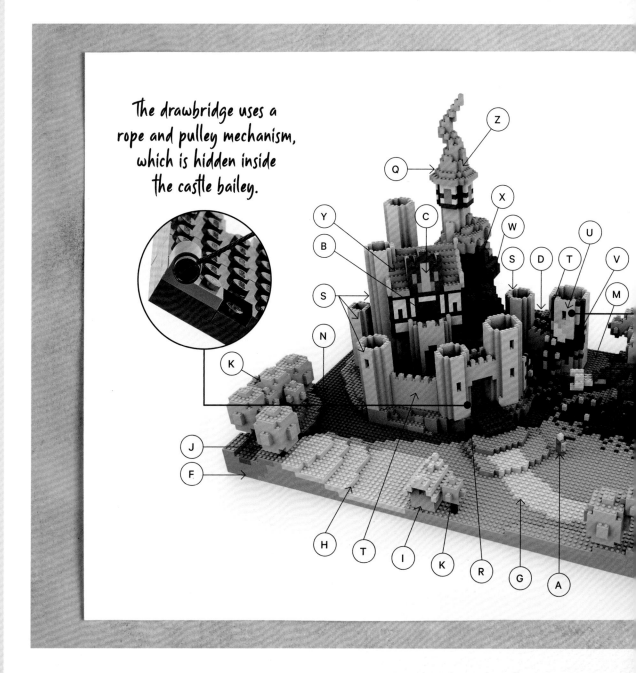

The drawbridge uses a rope and pulley mechanism, which is hidden inside the castle bailey.

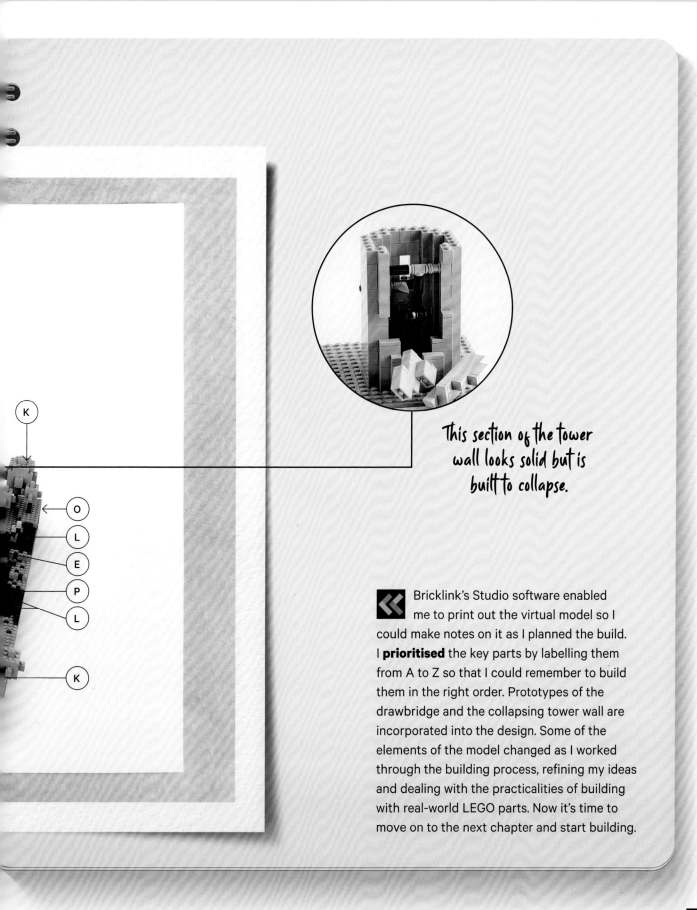

This section of the tower wall looks solid but is built to collapse.

◀◀ Bricklink's Studio software enabled me to print out the virtual model so I could make notes on it as I planned the build. I **prioritised** the key parts by labelling them from A to Z so that I could remember to build them in the right order. Prototypes of the drawbridge and the collapsing tower wall are incorporated into the design. Some of the elements of the model changed as I worked through the building process, refining my ideas and dealing with the practicalities of building with real-world LEGO parts. Now it's time to move on to the next chapter and start building.

FORM AND STRUCTURE

2

Who doesn't love a **TUMBLING TOWER** of bricks? An exploding moon base that showers the bad guy with fragments of a spaceship? Who isn't into a LEGO® fire station **BURSTING** into flames because the chief firefighter left their toast in the toaster? We all love to see stuff **COME APART** … sometimes. This chapter is all about making a build **SOLID** right from the beginning, so it only comes apart if you want it to.

A STURDY FRAME

Any LEGO build needs to be able to support itself without breaking apart or sagging. Taller models shouldn't sway violently and fall over. Larger models will need more elaborate support structures to ensure they don't collapse under their own weight. Planning a structure for the interior of your model, much like any type of building, will ensure that it is safe and sturdy and ready to take on all your crazy ideas!

Make a nice strong skeleton through your model and cover it up with the surface structure. Even though the outside of your model might be detailed and voluminous, the skeleton inside that supports it all can be as simple as you like. Make it square and brace it so it's supporting what it needs to. Nobody will see the interior supports of your model, so it doesn't have to be pretty, just strong.

> When you're designing a large model, time spent designing the support structure will actually speed up the building process. A good structure will minimise any accidents, not only for safety, but also so you don't waste time rebuilding, rehashing and redesigning.

Look at the plans for your model or a maquette (see page 32) and work out a simple, strong structural shape that you will build the model around. The basic structure doesn't have to follow every bump and curve, but essentially cuts a direct path through the model to connect it together.

Planning your internal structure beforehand can also help you to determine how you'll actually achieve some of the connections between features of the model. It gives you an idea in advance of how difficult or easy this may be to do. The basic structure of a model doesn't have to follow every bump and curve of the surface; it should be a few studs smaller in every direction than the outer shape you want to create, but with studs or other connections built in so that you can securely connect it to the exterior.

Think of what you need to prioritise in your structure as well: what is important for you to build first; what should be left until last; and in what order things need to be done in between. Try to see where sections overlap others and need to be added later. If something slots into something else, build the slot first. Like a puzzle, figure out how it should go together (see **Skill 1: Design and Prepare**).

> **A model should be like a beehive and not a sandcastle: it should be strong and solid, not fragile and crumbly.**

Here is the inside of
a mountain: because it
will be hidden, you can
use bricks of any colour.

SUPPORT

Once the internal structure for your model is in place, you can begin to think about any additional structures in the model and how they will be supported. Sometimes you want a brick-built section or element to appear to float above the surface, but because it's made from LEGO bricks it will most likely be heavy. To give the illusion of weightlessness, you'll have to find a way to support the structure without overengineering it. Big, obvious pylon supports won't make something look light and fragile. The solution can be as simple as shifting elements of your design until they have at least three points of contact with the framework of the model, so you can put more support structures in place.

Say that you want to have a clown holding a balloon. The balloon will be heavy, but thick supports underneath it will spoil the illusion. Placing a thin 1x1 'string' support directly under the balloon's centre of gravity will help, but if you then position the balloon so that it just touches the clown's hat in two places, you can also build a good amount of support through the intersecting areas. The heavy balloon is now supported in a way that's not immediately obvious to the observer, and you don't have to make the 'string' support underneath any thicker. To the observer, the LEGO balloon appears to be floating.

Back view: you can see where the balloon is connected to the clown's hat.

From the front, the balloon looks as though it's floating on top of the LEGO string.

1 Triangulate corners with diagonal bracing.

2 Connecting more than one stud prevents leaning.

BRACING

Take a tip from the world of engineering: to strengthen a structure, you can't allow it to lean in any direction. The way this is usually done is with bracing. So brace yourself!

1 The simplest type of bracing is to triangulate the corners. Instead of making squares that can pivot at the corners, brace them across the diagonal to prevent the uprights from leaning over. There aren't a lot of nice, neat triangles among LEGO parts so you would probably do this more often in larger structures.

2 Doubling the number of studs that are connecting at right angles will help to stop any leaning as well. A two-stud join will be sturdier than a single-stud join and will prevent pivoting.

3 If you need to make the inner structure sturdy, make sure to cross your supports with at least two-stud wide bricks. This sturdy crisscrossed pattern is an excellent way to not only make a strong interior structure, but also to make the model light and easy to move without twisting. This works vertically as well as horizontally.

4 Bracing can also be done vertically with bracket pieces or SNOT bricks (see **Skill 4: SNOT**). Using brackets to clamp together vertically stacked pieces with a plate or brick studded sideways between the brackets is a lot sturdier than stacked bricks alone. The sideways studded parts stop the vertical bricks from separating.

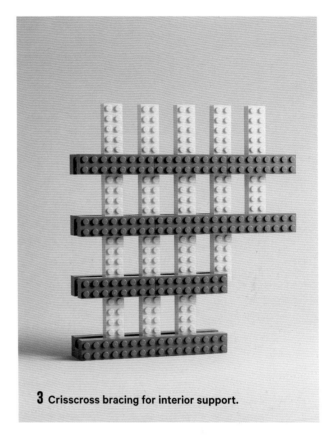

3 Crisscross bracing for interior support.

4 Brackets allow SNOT techniques to be used.

STRENGTH

When you want to make LEGO builds strong, the more connections the better, and when you need to make sure something is securely attached to something else, stud connections are the way to go. Overlapping pieces with stud connections is a good way to reinforce large sections of LEGO bricks.

Overlapping several layers of LEGO bricks by two or more studs will help to strengthen long sections. The more layers that overlap by significant amounts, the more strength. It is also a good idea to stagger where the bricks join so there is not a clear 'fault line' in the bricks where the build can come apart. Bricks can also be replaced with plates so you get even more overlapping in a small area to make things stronger. The only drawback is that layering plates will also make the area denser and, therefore, heavier (see *Weight*, page 54).

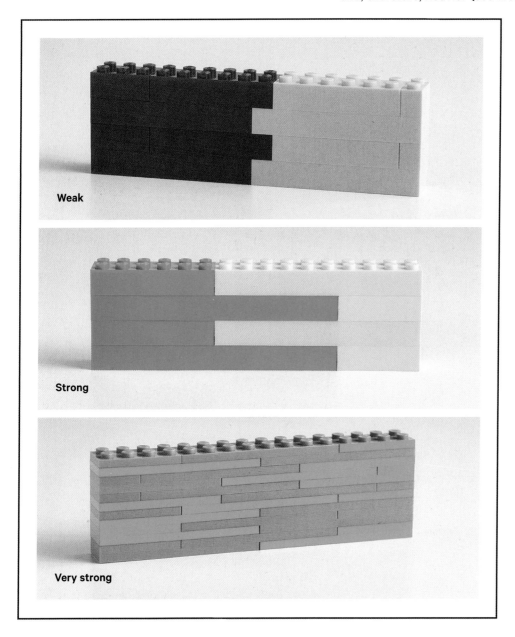

Weak

Strong

Very strong

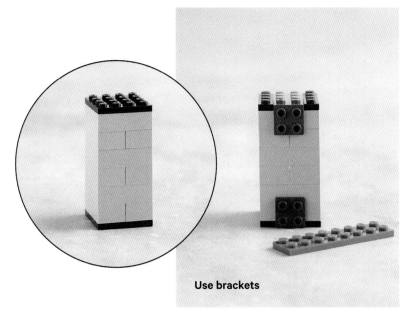

Use brackets

Connect with long plates

Add opposite brackets

There are now studs in three directions

Studs can only be pulled apart in one direction, so increasing the number of planes (sides) that have stud connections will add strength. The example here has bricks with additional brackets connected by a long plate. There are now connections on two different planes. You can add another set of brackets and plates opposite the first; this piece now has studs on three different planes, so trying to pull it in any direction will pull against something else.

Weak

Strong

Very strong

 In the same way that adding more stud connections make the joins stronger, connecting sections with multiple numbers of clips, ball joints, pins and bars will do the same thing. You can attach a section of your model with one clip and it might stay in place, but two clips will balance and even it out; anchoring it with four or more clips will make it even sturdier. Increasing the number of connection points will strengthen the join.

If you are joining or bridging areas, longer LEGO pieces can be handy too. A 16-stud-long brick (or plate) is available in a variety of colours. Use enough overlap to make the bracing sturdy. They can be built into the middle of the section, and if the available colours don't match your palette, they are effectively buried inside the structure.

Make a bridge and build over it.

WEIGHT

One problem you'll come across as you design and build bigger and better models is how heavy they might end up. A solid model will be strong, but it also may be quite heavy, which could make transporting or moving it difficult. Larger models will obviously be heavier than smaller ones, but that doesn't mean they should be impossible to lift.

When you are making brick-built human figures, the head becomes precarious, as it's a large heavy section at the top of the model. Because the thinner neck is usually the only support, the head can frequently break off, especially when the model is moved. We don't want that!

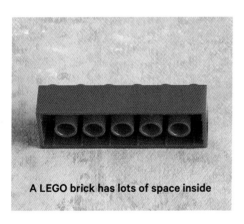

A LEGO brick has lots of space inside

Stacked plates are more solid

One good way to reduce the weight is to hollow out large sections as you would a jack-o'-lantern pumpkin. The outer surface can be as detailed and bumpy as you like, built as a shell, but if you omit most of the interior it will be a lot lighter. The only problem with a shell is that it isn't very strong, as there is nothing to stop it from collapsing inwards. To support a shell, the interior should be an overlapping crisscrossed structure, so even though it is mostly hollow it still has something to support it.

Another way to make a large model easier to lift and carry is to make it modular. That way, individual sections can be split into smaller parts. 'Slicing' a design of large, continuous forms into sections can make it easier to set up, transport and move around. For example, if you're building a spherical planet, you might make it in segments – halves or quarters – that can easily be separated and reassembled elsewhere.

Layering plates will add to the strength, but it will also add to the weight. Several plates that take up the same space as a brick are denser: bricks are mostly hollow, while plates are mostly solid plastic. In the same way, a lot of very small pieces will add more to the overall weight than a larger piece taking up the same space. There's a choice between what you consider important – strength or lightweight construction – and you'll need to decide what is more important in any situation.

A hollow sphere with
crisscross bracing inside
is lighter than a solid ball
of LEGO bricks.

BALANCE

Nobody wants their model to fall over: there's crashing and smashing, and it's just no fun. A fallen model means clean-up and reconstruction. To ensure that your model won't teeter or tip over, you need to make sure that it has good balance.

Tall models need extra thought about how to keep any extensions balanced around the centre of gravity.

>> In the design stage, think about how your model is balanced and which parts will potentially be heavy enough to pull the model over. Tall sections require a big enough base so they won't sway and topple. If you are worried about the balance of the model, do some tests by making a maquette (see page 32), and see how that stands up. Moving heavy sections, or the supports for those sections, towards the middle of the model will change the centre of gravity and hide the extra support structures. Remember that gravity pulls down on heavy sections, so if a heavy section is off-centre, the model will be pulled over in that direction.

Use a wide base and a solid vertical section to maintain the centre of gravity in the middle of the build.

If you are balancing something that needs to look precarious, you can counterbalance it by adding more weight to the opposite side. This can be done with LEGO bricks by making the counterbalance denser, using plates, filling the interior or adding weights. If you prefer to only use LEGO pieces in your builds, there are LEGO weights (normally used for trains and boats) available.

1 Connecting the model to a solid base using studs is a good start, but if it's still off-balance it can easily pull away from the base. Studding it down in several places will make it much harder for the model to pull away from all of the contact points. It's a good idea for any model to have at least three contact points with the base or ground, like a tripod: having more than two legs prevents the model from leaning too far in any direction.

2 Ensuring that a model has no wobbly or loose connections is a great way to prevent it from swaying. Looseness leads to wobbliness, wobbliness leads to swaying, swaying leads to leaning and leaning leads to tipping, crashing and smashing. Using other techniques from this chapter can help you to add sturdy, well-connected, lightweight sections to your model that won't increase the wobbliness and swaying.

3 If the model is tall and has no place to attach supports to balance it, consider making a large base for it and run support up through this. If you are making a building or a tree, you could add some landscape beneath it. If you are making a long-legged alien or a dinosaur, its feet could spread out a little further to make a wider base for it to stand on. Think about your subject and an appropriate ground or object that could be attached to its footing for balance.

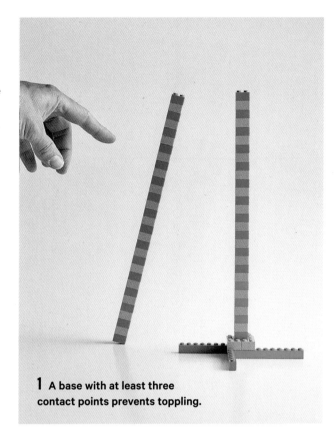

1 A base with at least three contact points prevents toppling.

2 Even if everything is tightly connected, it will be likely to fall over if it's top-heavy.

3 Spread the feet out over
a wide area for support.

LEVEL UP

Ensuring the stability and balance of your model may mean that you need to take your LEGO skills to the next level, and use some of the special pieces produced by the LEGO Group, such as SNOT (Studs Not On Top) bricks, brackets and LEGO Technic™ parts, which are designed to brace against movement. There's plenty more on these skills in later chapters; they are invaluable in helping to make stronger structures from LEGO parts.

SNOT

If someone says that their model is held together with SNOT, don't worry; this doesn't mean they've used the contents of their nose as a makeshift glue. SNOT is the not-at-all-gross use of bricks with studs on the sides. SNOT bricks are used a lot in building when you need to add detail to the side of a build, but can also be used to add strength to a structure. SNOT bricks running up the side of a build can be braced (see page 49) with plates. This effectively clamps the bricks together as they can't separate vertically, pushing against the plates.

When making a structure you may wonder about a good way to change the direction of the structure while still keeping it nice and strong. This is another use for SNOT bricks and brackets. If the section also has SNOT bricks, you can brace it all together with plates running from the original section across the join to the added section. These can be quite strong. (See **Skill 4: SNOT** for more.)

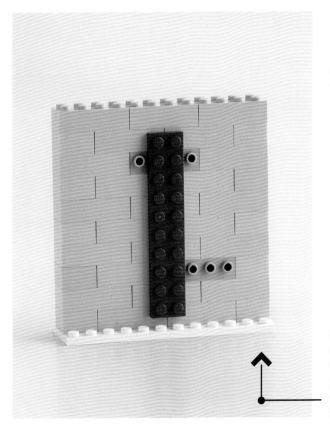

Including SNOT stud connections on the side of your build means you can add plates for bracing and you can also build off those studs in a perpendicular direction.

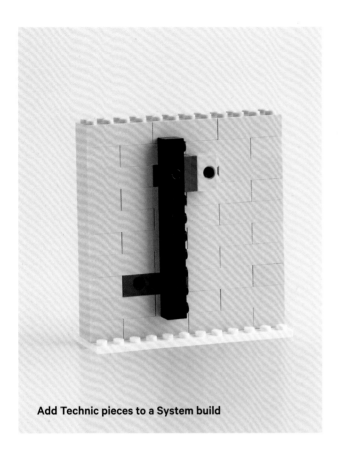

Add Technic pieces to a System build

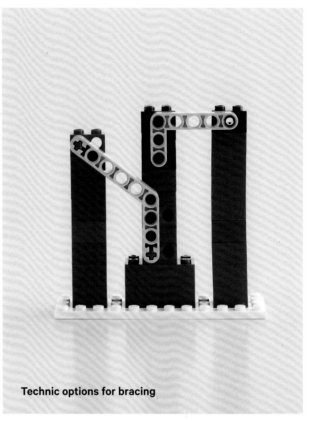

Technic options for bracing

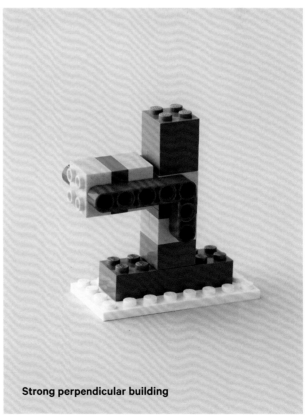

TECHNIC FRAMES

Adding LEGO Technic parts to your structures can give extra functionality and achieve things that are harder to do with regular LEGO System bricks. As with SNOT bricks, you can add long Technic pieces to System bricks to strengthen the structure. Unique Technic angled beams can be used to 'bend' your structures in ways that make them sturdy; this would be harder to achieve with regular System parts. Angled beams can also be used as bracing for perpendicular sections branching off a vertical build.

Strong perpendicular building

SMOKE AND MIRRORS

Even though a solid structure for the model is important, you don't want to lose the illusion of the genuine article. You want the observer to be able to suspend disbelief: if they are transported to a world where a dragon can fly, but they see a thick pole holding it up, the illusion is shattered. You can use any of the following techniques to conceal pieces of structure, joins and connections that are too obvious. These are metaphorical 'smoke and mirrors'.

BURY

≫ A great way to conceal structure is to bury it. If you need to do something structural and the whole of the structure can be inside the model, an observer will never know it's there. This is a favoured method as there is no extra outside building. It also means you don't have to worry about detailing the structure or what colours you use. If your structure needs pieces that don't come in model-matching colours, it doesn't matter when the observer can't see it.

> Clever use of LEGO parts to hide solid structure can seem like magic, but it's all sleight of hand.

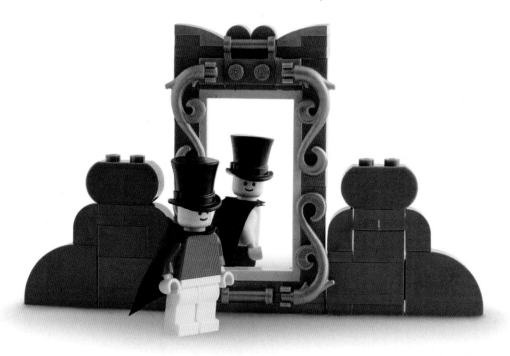

The flat join between these two sections is strengthened with Technic parts and then covered so the joint won't be noticed.

The stacked plates with studs up add varied height and texture to appear as a continuous grassy slope.

COVER

Quite often when you join sections of models together, they come with edges: obvious break lines between the sections. These can be concealed simply by covering them with something else. Ask yourself what could usually be found around that intersection of the build. It could be anything you can think of as long as it makes sense in that space. Natural landscape cover – like grass, plants, trees, bushes, groundcover, a pond, rocks or logs – is a good option. You could cover a join with minifigures in action: working, playing, resting, travelling or doing anything you like. You could cover it with a feature, such as a building, a fountain, a worker's hut, a parked vehicle, a statue, a fence or wall, a garden bed, an electrical box or a sleeping dragon. If the model is something other than a landscape, you can cover the joins with things that make sense for the subject: for example, cover an animal with fur, scales, fins or feathers; if it's a spaceship, add an access port, a radar dish, an airlock or a spacey gizmo.

This angled joint would be quite obvious, but studs-up plates add a rough texture and blend the join effectively.

It's all smoke and mirrors: from the surface, you can't see how the angled sections are connected.

BLEND

Blending a join is easier than you think. It's not literally melding the LEGO parts together, but breaking up the solid straight lines of the join. This can be achieved by making one side of the join slide over the top of the other. The covering edge is staggered in a fringe-like way or detailed so the straight-line join becomes a crooked one, making it harder to discern. This also works when there are angled gaps between sections. (For more ideas on adding texture to a surface, see also *Greebles*, page 200.)

> If all else fails, cover the join with a minifig like me!

DISGUISE

If you can't hide the internal structure or blend the joins, then the next best thing is to try disguising them. Make any structure that needs to be on the outside of the model look like it is something else that is supposed to be there.

If you are trying to disguise a join or structural element in the model, make a feature of it: a change in colour, texture or material. Structure can be disguised by adding details in the 'scene' of your model, such as a column of smoke, an artfully placed piece of vegetation, or a flowing piece of costume to disguise the supporting column. Sometimes details can be disguised simply by putting something nearby that is more interesting, so the observer is distracted by the detail. This doesn't mean you shouldn't try to conceal the join or structure as much as you can, but redirecting attention away from it is a great way to add to the disguise.

The connection between the arm and the sleeve is disguised by the change in texture and detail, which distracts you from how it's done.

A plane appears to be flying through clouds, which disguise the structure that holds the plane in place.

FOCAL POINTS

Just as you need to break any big build into manageable shapes or chunks in order to tackle them, you should also think about what features you'd like to focus on and add detail to. Spend time mapping out how these sections will attach to the whole, and what kind of base, frame or skeleton your model will be built on (see *Using a SNOT skeleton base*, page 100).

 Choose the areas of your build that will be the focal points – the areas where you can see parts of the story you're telling (see **Skill 5: Telling a Story**) or that really are the key to making the build recognisable – and start with them. Make sure that the rest of the model will support these features and draw attention to them rather than distract from them. Spend time mapping out the shapes and getting the right parts and techniques worked out so that you're happy with them. The majestically tall pillars and ornate pediment on the building pictured opposite draw the eye down towards the minifig tycoon at their base, while symmetrically placed lamps and planter boxes also focus attention on the central figure.

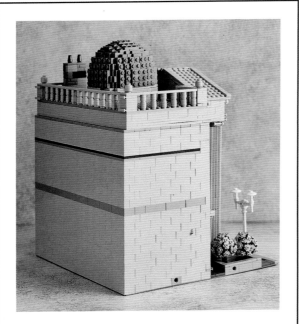

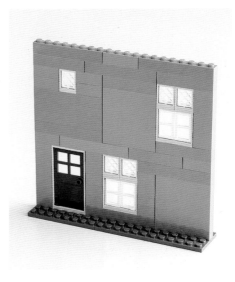

Other areas of the build don't necessarily require as much attention and therefore can be built more simply, using larger bricks or panels, and with less fine detail.

There's no point building details on the back of a structure, or creating a detailed interior, if no one is going to see them. These sections should be as simple as possible: try to use larger bricks or panels to minimise the parts usage, or just use parts you know you have lots of. Be careful not to forget the lessons learned in this chapter: even though something won't be seen, it still needs to be strong and connected to any internal structure.

Place the important details
where they will be seen.

BRICKMAN'S CASTLE BUILD

FROM THE BOTTOM UP

» To create **a sturdy frame** for the castle, I needed to work out how to **support** the structure with a strong skeleton. I considered the **strength**, **weight** and **balance** of the model. From a firm and solid horizontal base, vertical walls and the structures that are perpendicular to them required **bracing** for stability, as any movement would place stress on the LEGO joints and could cause the model to break apart or collapse under its own weight.

Prioritisation

The bottom of the castle moat is the lowest point in the model, so the first thing I did was to lay down the black bricks to mark out its position on the baseplate. Once that was in place, I could start on the structure of the whole model. With the base layers of the internal skeleton in place, the next step was to lay down the plates and bricks for the castle grounds.

Cross-bracing

I used this opportunity to begin placing the coloured bricks that will form the outer walls of the model: brown earth, grey stone and green grass. With all the structures I had in mind, it was going to be quite heavy, so I wanted to make sure that the internal support started at the very base of the build. Even the flat areas of ground outside the castle walls needed support.

SOLID STRUCTURE

>> Once the base structure of cross-braces and framing bricks was down, I began building the terrain on top, starting with layers of bricks. When building terrain like this, it can be useful to look at topographic maps, which show different levels of altitude (height) as concentric shapes. Each shape's outline represents a certain height, and the closer the lines are together, the steeper the incline. Building terrain with LEGO bricks works in much the same way.

Get the levels right with the bricks first, then smooth the transitions from level to level with layers of plates.

Smoke and mirrors

Using staggered edges and scattered colours to create texture is a way of visually **blending** the edges of the layers to create the illusion of a continuous smooth slope in the castle grounds.

Large creatures like the kitten and dragon need solid frames and sections built with Technic and SNOT to hold their poses and allow details to be added later.

BRICKMAN'S CASTLE BUILD

Cross-bracing

Crisscrossed LEGO parts for internal bracing can be in any colours you have available, as it will all be hidden by the terrain or building around it. In the area under the castle I made the cross-bracing stronger to help support the eventual weight of the castle.

Modularity

It's at this stage that I built in solid connections that will hold the finished modules of the castle together securely.

Solid base

On areas of terrain where colours change a lot or I needed to add detail in the form of lots of smaller bricks, I made a solid platform of bricks or plates, which gave me the flexibility to place pieces where they were needed.

SCALE AND SHAPE

3

This skill set is complex, but mastering it will be rewarding and will set you up to take your models to the next level, using the **GEOMETRY OF LEGO® BRICKS**. Try the techniques in this chapter a few times in **DIFFERENT WAYS**, remembering that there is no single right way to do something, but rather billions of opportunities for you to **ACHIEVE YOUR BUILD GOALS**.

SCALE

The easier part of the scale and shape equation is to figure out just how big or small your LEGO model will be: this is the 'scale' conundrum. Will your model have minifigs in it, or will you be creating a large brick-built character? Will you build something 'life size'? How many bricks do you have? Do you have enough of the right colour? Your answers to these questions and more will impact the choice of scale for your build.

Building your model larger than life allows you to represent very fine details using LEGO parts.

RATIOS

Scale is usually measured and represented by a ratio: two numbers with a colon between them. The first number is almost always 1, to represent 1 unit (usually 1 cm or 1 inch) and the second number is the 'real world' dimension it represents. So 1:1 means 1 cm in the model equals 1 cm in real life; in other words, the model is 'life size'. A scale often used in LEGO builds is 1 LEGO stud equals 30 cm (12 inches) in real life, which equates approximately to a scale of 1:43 (where 1 cm on the model equals 43 cm in real life).

helmet. The main issue with this scale, though, is that it makes minifigs effectively 1.2 metres (4 feet) wide (measured across their arms and torso), which is much wider than most real people.

An alternative is to scale things based on the minifigs' heads. Just as with real people, you tend to look at a minifig's face and head first, and this is what gives a model life and draws focus, so it makes sense that if the rest of the model scales to the minifigs' heads, it will seem more proportionate (see *Proportion*, page 82). Using this method, the scale comes out close to 1:30.

MINIFIG SCALE

The most common scale used for LEGO sets is 'minifig scale'. But what does this mean? Minifig scale isn't exact and varies depending on how you want to interpret or use it. Typically, it ranges between 1:25 and 1:50. The simplest solution is to decide how tall your minifigs are supposed to be and then use that to measure how big everything around them should be. Using the 1 stud:30 cm (12 inches) scale makes most minifigs around 160–180 cm (5–6 feet) tall, depending on their hairpiece, hat or

PARTS SCALE

Another way to scale your model is to choose a key part of the model and find a LEGO part (or parts) that represent it accurately. It could be as straightforward as the door of a house (using standard LEGO doors) or the wheel of a vehicle (LEGO wheels and tyres come in a LOT of different sizes, but some may more accurately represent what you're building). The main advantage of this method is that LEGO parts you already have will dictate the scale and make your LEGO build more achievable.

Minifig scale is not super-realistic but it's an easy way to determine the size of a model.

The scale of this dinosaur's head is
dictated by the curved fang pieces
and pentagonal tiles used as scales.

PROPORTION

After scale, the next most important decision to make with your LEGO model is proportion. Proportion means how the model scales internally; that is, how different parts of the model scale to each other. The key to making proportion work for a model is consistency and recognisability: if you're representing a giraffe, then it needs to have long legs and a long neck for people to recognise it.

>> That said, a common technique used in larger models is 'selective compression'. This means building the focal points of a model (see page 68), or areas that interact with minifigs, at a consistent scale, but then selectively choosing other aspects of the model to compress or make smaller to save on room and bricks (see also *Selective compression*, page 26).

This giraffe's proportions are not quite right, although it is recognisable because the important features are all present.

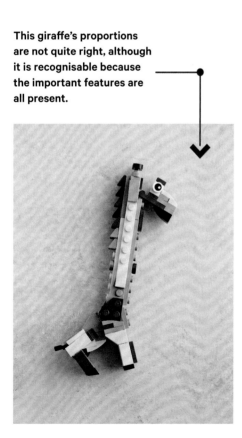

In this model of Grauman's Chinese Theatre, Hollywood, the box office section (between the forecourt and the cinema) has been compressed to save space and materials.

SHAPE

Now that you have figured out the scale of your build, it's time to move on to the hardest part, the shape. This is often a more tedious part of the build, as just working out the shapes involves very little detail work, and sometimes you need to spend time on parts of a LEGO model that won't ever be seen. For example, let's say you want to make a MOC (My Own Creation) of some Sherpa minifigures climbing up Mount Everest. Even though it's about the minifigures and their cool expressions, you still need to build the giant shapes of the mountains they are climbing on, otherwise the story won't show how awesome those minifigures are.

Every model, no matter what it is – from a spaceship to an elephant – can be broken down into a series of basic shapes. Once you understand how to build those basic shapes, you can join them together, and start doing all the fun things like details and theming.

Sometimes the iconic shape of your subject will be hard to replicate with LEGO bricks because it is organic, or textured in a way that's not conducive to being made out of little rectangular bricks. If it has any type of intricate detail or smooth curves it becomes a challenge to reproduce.

So how do you deal with something made up of multiple shapes, or unusual shapes? The easiest way to tackle anything difficult is to break it down into manageable chunks and deal with each part separately. That way you have smaller problems that you can solve individually and then integrate into the larger build to make the whole thing more achievable.

BASIC SHAPES

Observe the overall shape of the object you want to make and break it down into simpler shapes. See if there are obvious shapes you can recognise in your subject, such as rectangles, squares, cubes, triangles, pyramids, cones, circles, ovals, cylinders, spheres, domes, etc. You may also identify more complex shapes: peanut, doughnuts, stars, teardrops, capsules, sausages, bananas, hearts, pie pieces, and so on.

Some of these shapes will be easier to make than others: rectangles and squares are easy; spheres, circles, oblongs and angled geometric shapes are harder; and irregular organic shapes are the hardest. Difficult shapes will take some ingenuity and a combination of different techniques and specific pieces to achieve.

Think about the pieces that you have, plus the types of shapes that you know how to build and start with the easiest first. Then you can work on the shapes you aren't sure how to build and solve those separately. Much like an archaeologist piecing together a dinosaur skeleton from a pile of fossilised bones, you can start with the things you are most familiar with and work out the harder stuff later.

GRIDDING

▶▶ Using a grid is a great way to help understand the many shapes your model might have, and to start to think 'in the LEGO System' (see *LEGO resolution* and *LEGO maths*, page 114). A grid will reveal shapes that you can then tackle individually. The LEGO grid of studs and bricks can be used to advantage when designing and planning projects, including the layout of the model, designs on the model and the shape of the model.

Starting from the bottom up, a LEGO baseplate is the most useful grid for planning the size of a build. Each stud on the baseplate can correspond to a square on a grid, so it's easy to place your plans onto the baseplate.

Where the LEGO grid gets tricky is that horizontally it is built on a square grid, but vertically it has a different height-to-width ratio. The smallest LEGO brick, a 1x1, is slightly taller than it is wide, so you'll have to use a 1 x 1.2 grid to design anything in the vertical plane. If you use a regular square grid for vertical planning, the model will end up about 20 per cent taller than intended, looking stretched. There are samples of both horizontal (square) and vertical grids on pages 288–291. You can photocopy these as many times as you like, or use them as a guide to create your own grid in a computer drawing program.

Overlay a grid onto a picture or sketch of your subject to help you work out the shape and scale of it. Adjust the size of the grid so that it lines up with obvious and logical changes in the subject, such as shapes or colours. From here you can plan how to build, and you'll see if you need to make adjustments to your design to make it fit the grid better. You can draw the bricks and pieces you wish to use onto the grid to represent the shapes of your subject. (See also *Mosaics*, pages 206–211.)

Use a square (horizontal) grid for a top-down view or a 1 x 1.2 vertical grid for a front, back or side view.

In a scenario where you know the number of bricks wide and high you want the model to be and need to see how the subject fits into those dimensions, use a grid with a fixed number of squares and shrink or enlarge the image to fit the grid.

Alternatively, if you know the scale you want to use for the model you can overlay a grid to help you work out how many bricks will be needed, using LEGO maths (see page 114).

Once you have planned the model using a grid it will be easier to position the different sections of your design as you start to build, and to ensure that they fit together correctly. Having a grid that matches the scale of the baseplate will make the whole process a lot easier.

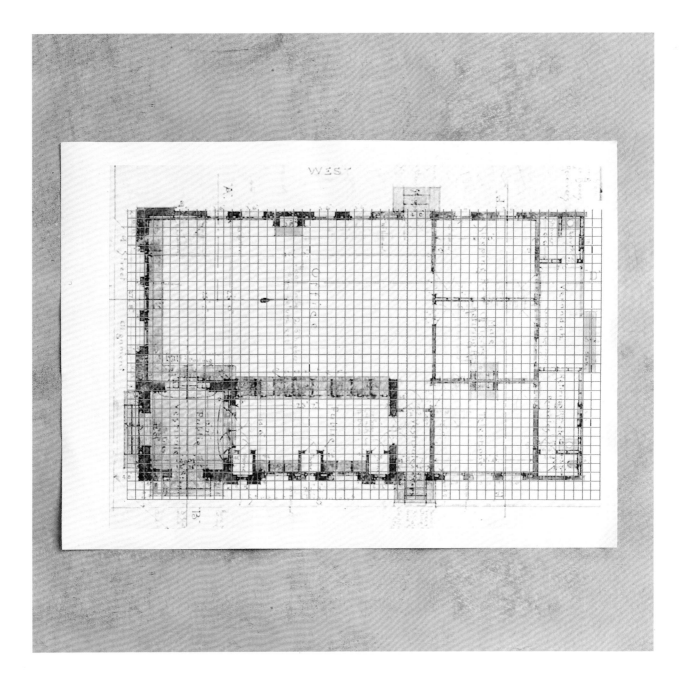

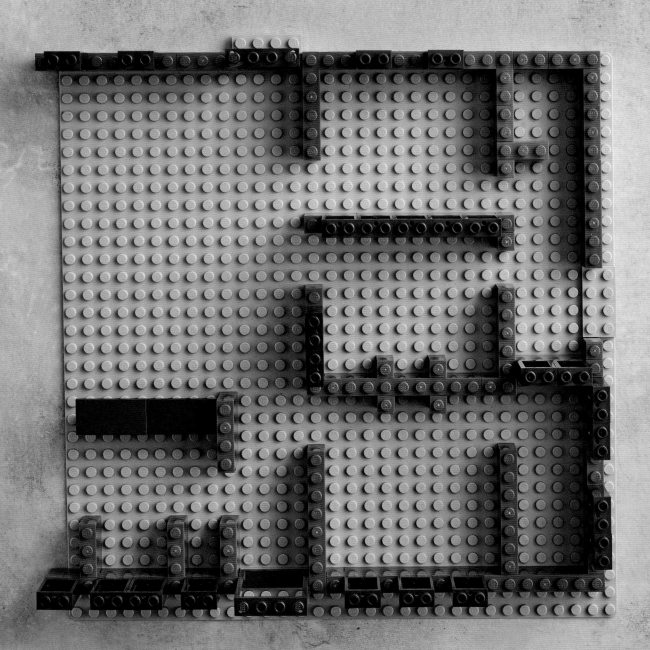

GEOMETRY

Now that you understand the way you can think about the LEGO System as one giant 3D grid, you can start to think about specific shapes and perhaps one of the biggest 'cheats' there is: when you only need to design half or even a quarter of a model because it is symmetrical. You simply design one half, then make the other half to match.

SYMMETRY

If you're trying to create any kind of regular shape, then symmetry comes into play. Symmetry is when both halves of something are mirror images. Many real objects, vehicles, buildings and creatures are symmetrical, so it pays to practise creating mirror images of a shape. Squares and circles, as well as many other shapes, are symmetrical.

>> Asymmetry is when the two halves of something DON'T match each other, as in our monster here. Apart from when you are re-creating naturally asymmetrical objects, such as trees or rocks, asymmetry can also be used to draw attention to a particular part of a model or to give something more character.

ANGLES

The first shape that you should master is triangles. Many more complex shapes can be achieved by combining triangles together. To tie into the LEGO System grid, it's easiest to create diagonals using standard angles and existing angular LEGO parts. 45 degrees is a common angle, but there are other angled parts available.

» Angles and diagonals are handy when you want to run diagonal sections off the regular grid of studs. Hinge plates are a common way to create these angles, but more recent parts, such as 1x2 plates with rounded ends, allow plates to pivot on a stud at almost any angle. Depending on the scale and angle of the diagonals, jumper plates (see page 94) can come in handy to link the diagonal back to the grid. Wedge plates and tiles make connecting angles into grids much easier; they are also good for disguising gaps (see *Cheese slopes*, page 125) made by builds going off-grid. Brackets, jumper plates, ball joints and clip hinges allow triangles to go in multiple directions and line up parts to create smoother diagonals.

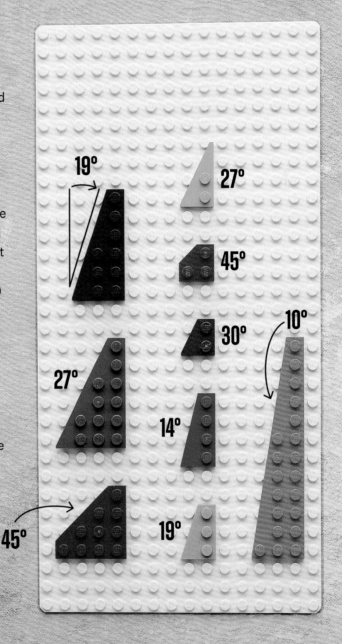

LEGO plates with angled edges can be used in any orientation.

CURVES

To create curves, you can radially attach parts from a central core, or use studs beneath the surface of the model that connect with hinges to create angles, even circles, that are hard to produce otherwise. This technique looks great on the outside, although the separate segments do not connect and the interior can be crowded with structure.

There are lots of sloped, angled, wedged and curved LEGO bricks you can use to vary the height and curve of the surfaces of your model. You can do this either horizontally across the studs or vertically up the faces. You can combine different angles to vary the slope pitch and effectively change the curve of the model.

1 Placing plates on angled studs gives even more options. Hinges, ball joints, clip joints and more are great ways to creatively position LEGO parts so that you can form the precise angles needed to achieve your model's shape.

2 Using curved sections on SNOT structures can give you more options than by building purely 'studs up'. The same interesting curves can also be added sideways or underneath.

3 It's possible to use a long chain of connecting 1x2 rounded plates to achieve a desired curve, and support its shape with an underlying structure. This can be good for smoothly undulating forms.

4 With sloped pieces alone you can make something appear curved, even though no curved pieces exist in the build. Depending on the pieces you use, you can create many irregular organic shapes that look effective.

1 Hinges create curves using flat plates.

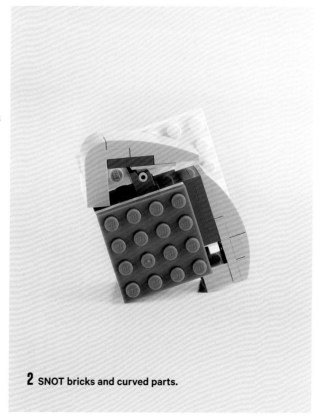

2 SNOT bricks and curved parts.

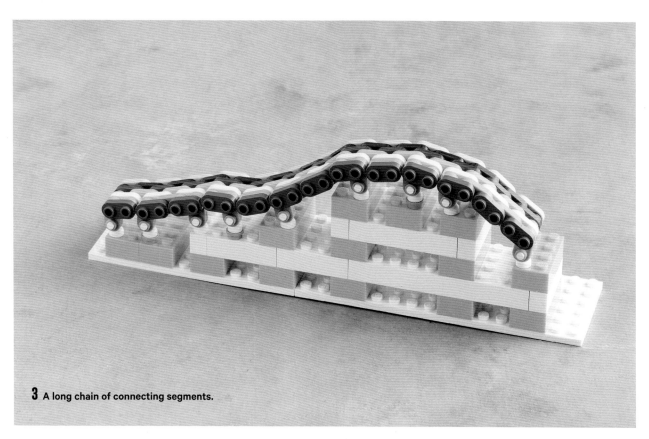

3 A long chain of connecting segments.

4 Slopes and wedges form curves.

JUMPING OFF THE GRID

One of the primary limitations of the LEGO system, when it comes to creating complex shapes, is the minimum size of its parts. Normally the smallest piece you can use is 1x1 stud by 1 plate in height; however, there are a few LEGO parts that enable finer details, effectively allowing you to 'jump off' the LEGO grid. The three most common parts that do this are jumper plates, brackets and headlight bricks. All of these parts enable you to offset the regular grid structure of the bricks and create more complex shapes than is normally possible with simple stacks of bricks, plates or slopes. See **Skill 4: SNOT** for a deep dive into how these parts can be integrated into models.

When you jump off-grid, keep in mind one thing: you will almost certainly need to connect the offset section back into the regular grid for stability.

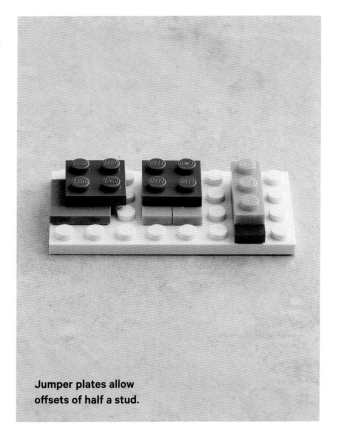

Jumper plates allow offsets of half a stud.

Jumper plates are LEGO plates that have their studs offset by half a stud in different directions from the normal grid of studs. They can be offset in line with the adjacent studs, or diagonally. Jumper plates were originally only available as 1x2 plates with a single centre stud, but these have since evolved into more variations that allow stronger and more versatile connections.

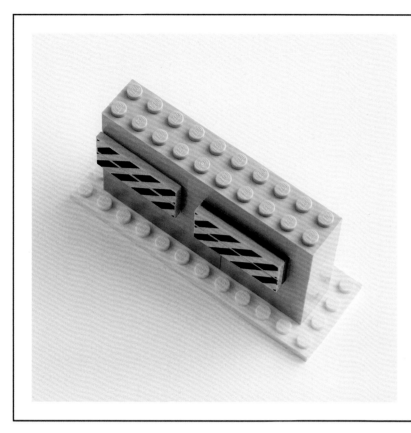

BRACKETS

≪ The thinner vertical areas of brackets are actually half a plate thick, which enables you to step a surface forward half a plate (you can see the black bracket behind the striped plates in the picture at left). Recent variations on the basic LEGO brackets, such as 1-stud wide brackets and more inverted versions, mean that these parts are even more versatile than before and can be used in smaller spaces or combined with other parts to create stronger builds.

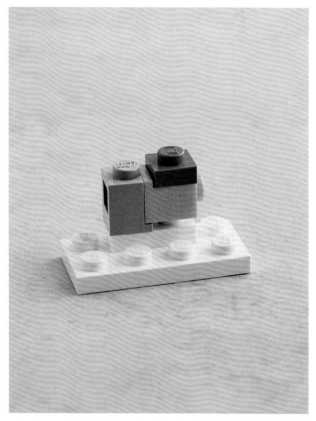

HEADLIGHT BRICKS

≫ Headlight or Erling bricks are some of the oldest and most versatile LEGO parts. The SNOT stud is recessed by half a plate-width, allowing you to step a surface back half a plate. Combined with this, they have an anti-stud on the opposite side of the brick, allowing them to accept studs horizontally. Read more about Erling bricks in **Skill 4: SNOT**. Here, attaching the yellow headlight brick to the grey one leaves you with a half-plate recess on the top of the structure. Adding the blue 1x1 plate gives you a half-plate step up.

OTHER TYPES OF OFFSETTING

Clips and bars offer a more flexible way to position parts, as clips can attach anywhere along a length of a standard LEGO bar or flextube; however, due to their size, they can be harder to integrate into a build without eating up space. Ball joints also allow more complex offsetting, but like clips and bars, the ball joint armature itself takes up a few studs of room and can be difficult to hide.

Clips, bars and flexible 4 mm hose are used to create complex brick-built wall decorations inset into a small sci-fi setting.

The back of the SNOT lettering (see pages 214–219) is attached using clips to a single bar and angled using a bar holder.

Vertical stripes following the curve are created by clipping them to a flexible hose, which is bent to and held in place with SNOT bricks at each end.

SILHOUETTES

When dealing with a complex shape it may be hard to understand the intricacies in the surface and underlying structure, and therefore to work out how to build the form. In this case it is worth looking at cross-sections of the object to see how its silhouette changes along its length. If the object is well-documented it might be possible to find cross-sections of it already posted online (depending on the subject matter) but otherwise you will have to make them yourself. This is usually done by observing, studying and sketching the shape until you can work out what its silhouettes would look like. You may find, after creating them the first time, that they still need tweaking to get them right. Once you have a good idea of them, you can start to build them in LEGO parts.

⏷⏷ Begin with the silhouettes of the front, top and side; this is often enough to get you started. You may need to deal with differing silhouettes along the length of an object, so using different cross-sections or slices of these shapes will help to merge them. Use as many as you need: the more complex the shape, the more of them may be necessary. Indeed, slicing a difficult object up like a big cake can help you to understand its form.

⏵⏵ Making these cross-section shapes and fitting them together in configuration can help you see how the form of a difficult object flows from one part to another. From there you will be able to imagine what fills the area between the slices and build what is needed to complete the model. Start with the easier, simpler sections, such as the head and torso of a body, that will help you visualise the rest and complete the harder ones.

Build up cross-sections in layers to mimic the desired silhouette. These are just placeholders, so the colours you use don't matter.

Complex shapes have
multiple silhouettes.

USING A SNOT SKELETON BASE

SNOT techniques are quite useful for making certain details and attaching odd shapes in awkward places (see **Skill 4: SNOT** for more examples). You may consider using SNOT techniques to make a shape that is not achievable with regular bricks and parts or a section that is otherwise hard to attach.

Create a frame to support your model that incorporates SNOT bricks, brackets, clips, bars or any other connection method. Then you can add shapes onto this frame to make the form increasingly complex. This is a good technique for making figures in dynamic poses, action figures, mech robots or any other complex subject.

>> Included in the internal structural skeleton, 1x1 SNOT bricks allow the addition of studded plates facing outwards, to form a base onto which horizontal extensions or decorative tiles can be attached.

Even the most complex SNOT
builds start with a simple base.

LOWELL SPHERES

Lowell spheres are a great way of using SNOT bricks and techniques to build in several directions from a single base. You don't have to stop at spheres: you can extend to making other shapes as well, such as eggs, doughnuts and sausages.

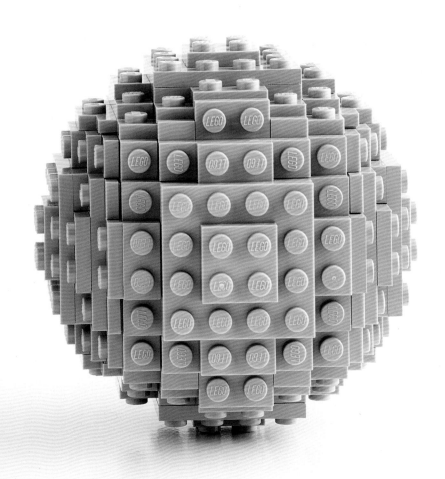

In 2002, Bruce Lowell developed this method of constructing a LEGO sphere using super Erling bricks (headlight bricks with studs on all four vertical sides) and flat plates.

Lowell egg

Doughnut

Sausage

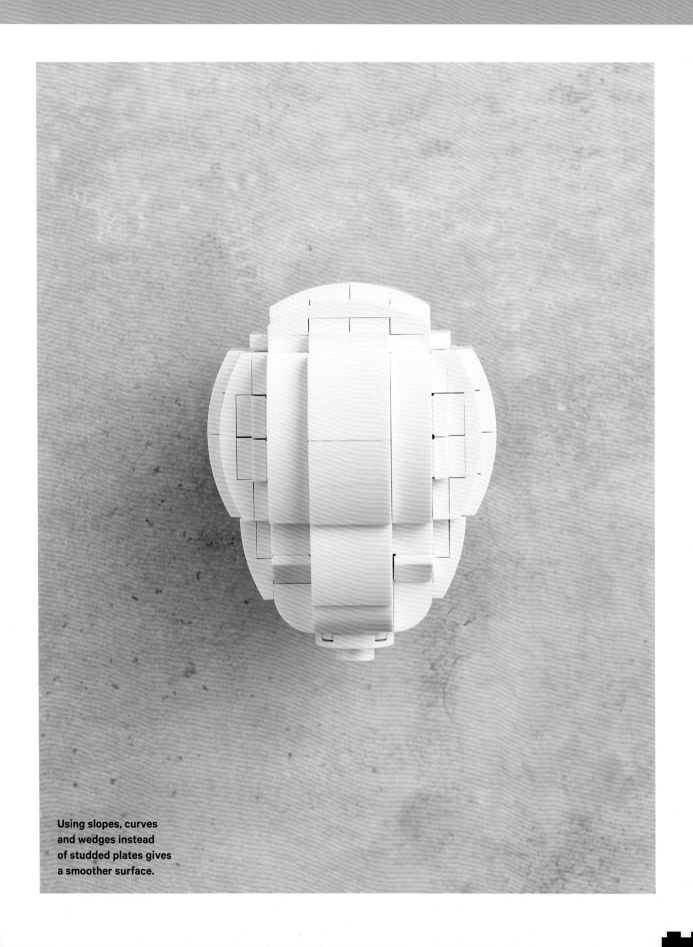

Using slopes, curves
and wedges instead
of studded plates gives
a smoother surface.

BRICKMAN'S CASTLE BUILD

SIZE AND SHAPE

The 48 x 48 and 32 x 32-stud base plates chosen for the segments of the castle model gave the **scale** for the castle, which is approximately 1:50 (minifig-scale). Because it is a cartoonish-style castle, I was less constrained to keep it in strictly realistic **proportion** and **shape**, which meant I could crowd all the structures around the keep inside the curtain walls.

After using a **grid** to plan the layout and work out the height of the towers, I started to look at the **geometry** of the build. The castle towers and walls were basically symmetrical, with small modifications for texture and interest. Cylindrical towers were planned using stepped bricks to create the **curves**. I built placeholder stacks of brightly coloured bricks into the shapes I wanted for the castle, to get the **silhouettes** right before I started building the real thing.

Building the slightly crooked and whimsical tower with its wonky hat required me to consider how to **jump off the grid**. The dragon and giant kitten were built up over **SNOT skeletons**.

The shapes of the undulating hills were built up over the supporting grid of bricks.

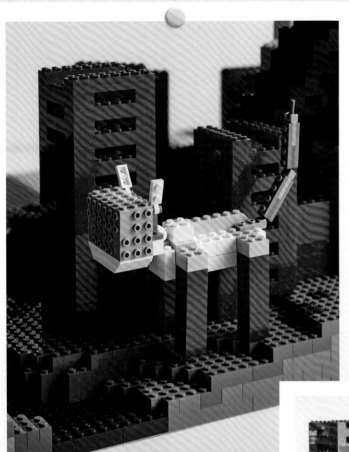

The giant kitten's size was mapped out using basic bricks and a SNOT core was designed for its head.

Silhouettes

Before I began actual construction of the castle towers and walls, I built quick stacks of multicoloured bricks to mimic the silhouettes and placed them so that I could get the buildings' sizes and proportions right.

BRICKMAN'S CASTLE BUILD

Curves

Building the castle's curvy silhouettes gave me a chance to check the stability of the twisty tower. I realised it would need extra support and designed a secondary structure (in black) that could be disguised as smoke from a fire.

Size

Building the castle and its grounds in sections meant that I could make it much larger without making it too heavy or unstable to move. (See also *Weight*, page 54.)

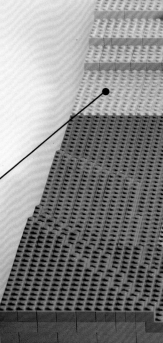

Scale

Knowing I was building to minifig scale gave me a limit on how big the dragon could be, which in turn dictated the parts I could use to give the dragon its shape.

SNOT

4

STUDS NOT ON TOP (SNOT) is one of the fundamentals of LEGO® building and really being able to push your limits: once you master the **POWER** of SNOT you are well on your way to the **INCREDIBLE**. SNOT is a broad term for a number of LEGO building techniques, in contrast to the original, and simplest, way of **CONNECTING** basic LEGO bricks and plates together, which is to connect the studs one on top of another.

SNOT BASICS

The earliest official SNOT techniques were used in LEGO sets in the early 1970s and involved wedging LEGO plates vertically between studs; however, it was soon decided that this put too much stress on the plate and could cause damage to the parts over time. One of the first dedicated SNOT elements, released in 1979, is known as an Erling brick, named after its inventor Erling Dideriksen. Also known as a 'headlight brick', because that's how it's commonly used in models, the versatility of this piece still comes in handy today. Since then, the LEGO SNOT element library has grown enormously and allows hundreds more SNOT connections that are more stable and versatile than ever before.

An Erling brick has an extra stud on one side and an anti-stud on the opposite side. It's also known as a headlight brick.

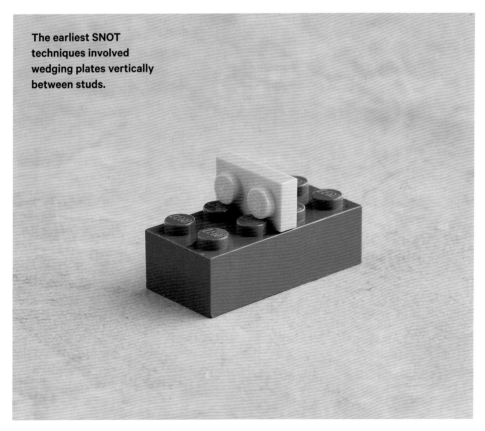

The earliest SNOT techniques involved wedging plates vertically between studs.

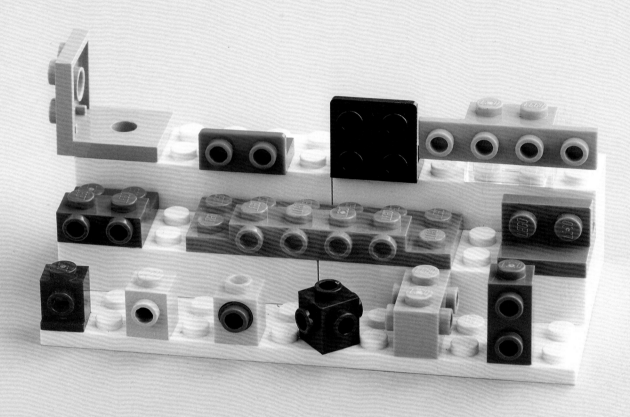

Modern SNOT elements come in many shapes and sizes, offering more stable and versatile LEGO connections.

For a long time, most SNOT elements were limited to a single-stud connection, meaning they were less stable, but the LEGO Group has released a wide range of elements with two or more studs facing in different directions, allowing for much stronger assemblies.

LEGO RESOLUTION

One of the primary uses of SNOT techniques is to improve resolution by making smaller steps in the LEGO grid, such as half-plate or half-stud spacing, as well as turning parts sideways or upside down to create shapes or patterns that can't be made when building straight up.

>> If you think of LEGO models as 3D pixel art, you can think of LEGO elements as pixels, or the basic units of image resolution. In this analogy, the smallest basic unit of brick and plate elements would be a 1x1 plate. This piece is the basis for the term 'F.L.U.', which stands for Fundamental LEGO Unit, and is essential for calculating LEGO maths.

There are other elements that have smaller effective resolutions, depending on which angle you view them from. LEGO bars, when viewed end on, form a small circle, but it's hard to integrate them into a shape. LEGO brackets, hinge tops and panel walls can form half-plate-thick lines when viewed sideways. Incorporating them can be hard too, especially when you effectively need to hide 90 per cent of the element.

> **Because LEGO parts follow a standardised building system based around LEGO bricks, maths is very useful, especially when you start using SNOT!**

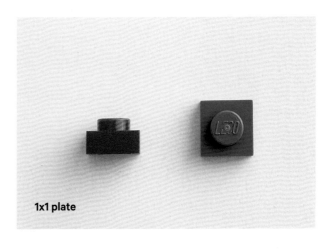

1x1 plate

LEGO MATHS

LEGO maths can help you calculate the number of bricks you need for a certain area, or how to make different sections of a model the same height. The main ratios you need to start with are:

- » 1 LEGO brick = 3 plates
- » 2 studs = 5 plates
- » 6 studs = 5 bricks
- » 1 stud wide = 2½* plates high

*The half-plate figure might sound scary, but it actually exists in quite a lot of LEGO elements! Notably, the thin section of a bracket is half a plate thick, and the good old headlight brick's side stud is inset half a plate back. Using these two elements together you can align all manner of SNOT shapes back to the regular LEGO grid.

1 brick = 3 plates

2 studs = 5 plates

6 studs = 5 bricks

1 stud wide = 2½ plates high

Erling (headlight) bricks and brackets

THE PERILS OF SNOT

As useful and amazing as the combinations that SNOT allows are, there are nevertheless some combinations that don't connect properly, even though you might think that they would!

The reason for this is LEGO tolerances. A 2-stud gap between bricks is 16 mm, but in reality a 1x2-stud brick or plate is actually 15.8 mm wide, with a 0.1 mm gap on each end. The LEGO parts need this tiny gap so that they can be easily removed. However, this gap only exists sideways, not vertically, because LEGO bricks are first and foremost designed to stack vertically, meaning that certain combinations of parts don't work when arranged sideways and this can cause small cracks and stresses in the build.

Placing these inverted 1x2 brackets with their studs going in opposite directions sounds like it should work, but their 0.1 mm tolerances are added together in the middle, meaning that they don't sit flush.

One of the few downsides to the otherwise versatile Erling brick (yellow) is that it doesn't have the 0.1 mm gap.

SNOT CONNECTIONS

As well as the versatility of dedicated SNOT bricks and brackets, there are other ways of making connections with specialised LEGO parts that enable you to build in multiple directions and at multiple angles. Some of these techniques are illustrated here.

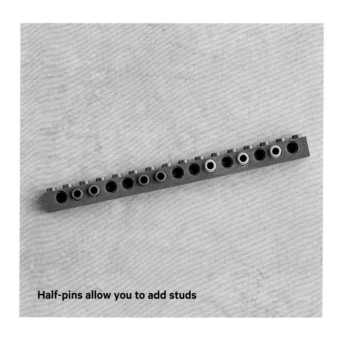

Half-pins allow you to add studs

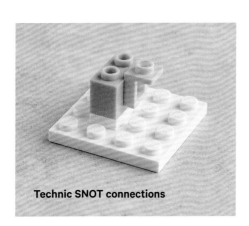

Technic SNOT connections

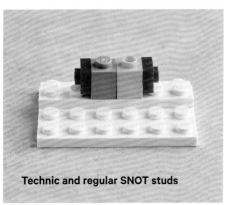

Technic and regular SNOT studs

TECHNIC AND SNOT

LEGO Technic™ bricks have long been used as SNOT elements. Because half-pins allow you to add studs anywhere you want along a Technic brick, they are very useful.

◀◀ But while you might think at a glance that a 1x1 Technic brick with a half-pin would be the same as a 1x1 SNOT brick, it actually isn't. The centre of a Technic half-pin is a tiny bit (0.12 mm to be exact) higher than a stud on a regular SNOT brick.

What this means is that you can't mix these two types of SNOT to connect the same assembly. You either need to use all SNOT bricks, or all Technic bricks with half-pins.

Another useful function of Technic bricks is the use of the pin holes as SNOT anti-studs. In this way a Technic brick can be used as a kind of reverse SNOT brick. Because Technic bricks' pin holes are usually offset to the studs on top, Technic bricks can be used to create SNOT half-stud offsets.

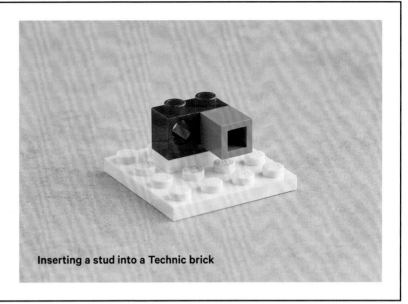

Inserting a stud into a Technic brick

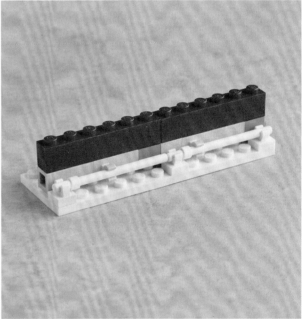

CLIPS AND BARS

One way the LEGO Group has begun to improve the versatility of SNOT techniques is the expansion of the range of clip-and-bar elements. A clip attached to a bar is stronger than a stud attached to the underside of a brick or plate, making clips and bars a better choice for stronger models, which should always be a priority for a LEGO product.

One of the primary advantages of a clip-and-bar assembly is that it can be attached anywhere along the length of a bar.

SIDEWAYS

Using SNOT elements to build sideways is the most common SNOT technique. Most official LEGO sets use this in at least one area of their builds and therefore there is an increasingly wide array of parts available to connect pieces sideways in very stable ways. By implementing the four LEGO maths ratios (see page 114) you can extrapolate how and when to use various SNOT elements to align studs so they are perpendicular to each other.

GRAVITY

>> The biggest danger for building SNOT in any direction is gravity. The further you go out from a studs-up stack, the more likely it is that your SNOT assembly will fall off. To combat this, you should try to use as many SNOT elements as possible to connect your sideways assembly securely back to the vertical structure.

Depending on the size of your sideways assembly you may also need to consider weight and balance (see **Skill 2: Form and Structure** for more detail).

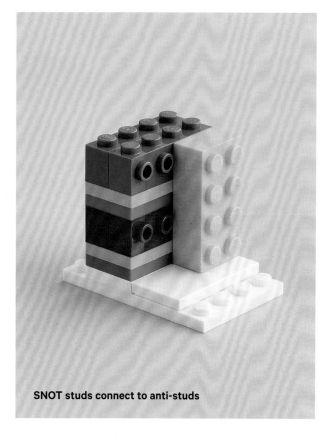

SNOT studs connect to anti-studs

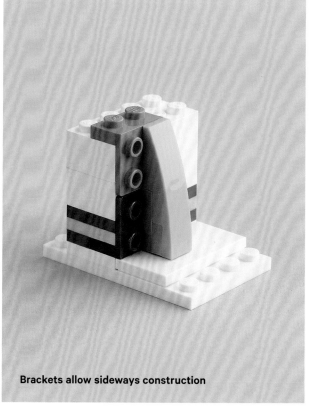

Brackets allow sideways construction

Use as many SNOT elements
as you can to connect your
sideways assembly back to
the vertical.

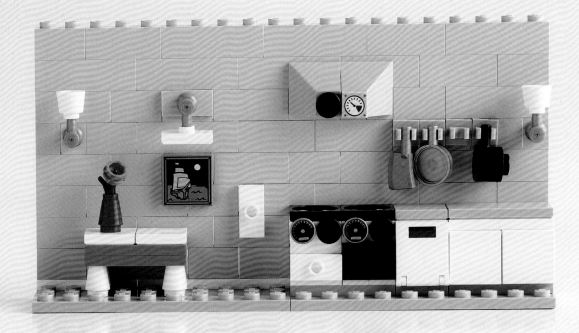

**Use SNOT to attach lamps
and other fittings to a wall.**

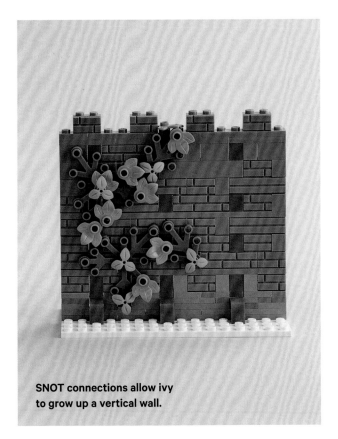

SNOT connections allow ivy
to grow up a vertical wall.

Curves can be created
using SNOT.

DETAILING

The most common use of SNOT is for attaching
simple details, such as a lamp, light switch or painting,
to a wall. Another great use for sideways SNOT is
adding texture to a vertical surface: mechanical
greebles on a spaceship surface or bricks on a house,
for example (see **Skill 6: Details**). You can line up
cheese slopes and cheese graters to create a straight
slope. Building sideways also allows you to create
more organic shapes such as curves, either by
attaching slopes sideways or by stepping out
sideways in bricks or plates.

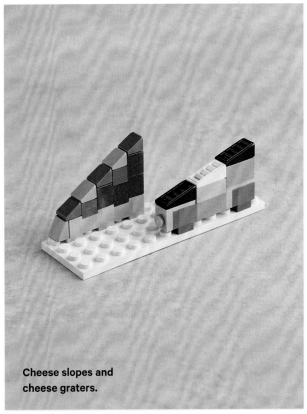

Cheese slopes and
cheese graters.

INSETTING

DECORATIVE DETAILS

Sideways SNOT is a great way to brick-build finer details into a flat surface, be it vertically stacked bricks, or a flat plate and tile surface. By insetting SNOT assemblies into a wall you can add stripes, fancy windows or even letters and words using the standard 2-stud-high SNOT alphabet (see *SNOT letters and numbers,* pages 214–219).

COVERING THE GAPS

When insetting, LEGO maths (see page 114) is important so that your SNOT assembly will sit comfortably on its base without gaps. You should cover the studded end of your sideways SNOT assembly with a tile, or have an anti-stud to accept it so that gaps are not seen.

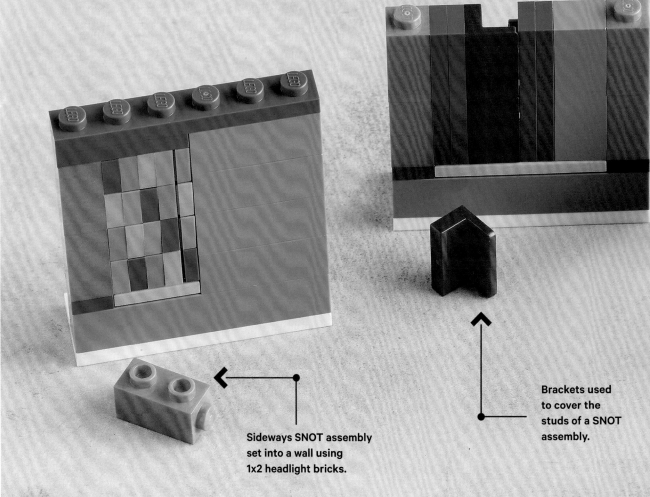

Sideways SNOT assembly set into a wall using 1x2 headlight bricks.

Brackets used to cover the studs of a SNOT assembly.

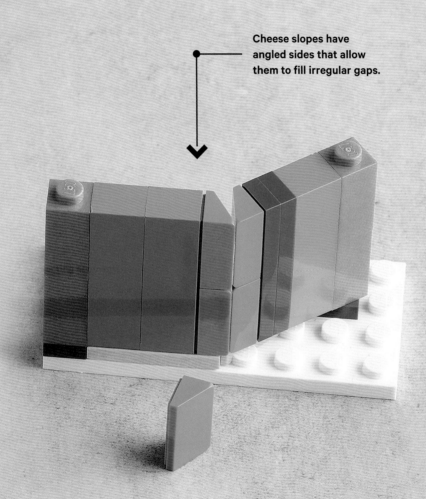

Cheese slopes have angled sides that allow them to fill irregular gaps.

CHEESE SLOPES

Panels and cheese slopes can be useful in filling or covering irregular gaps created when you inset SNOT sections. They have the benefit of both not having studs and only a thin edge, meaning they can hide messy connections.

UPSIDE DOWN

I f you can have studs going sideways, then you can also get your studs going upside down! There are a handful of LEGO elements that allow this, but the most common way is to turn a SNOT brick, which has studs on opposite sides, sideways. There are also a few older elements (no longer in production) that can create 180-degree stud reversals in less space. If you have room, you can combine brackets to reverse the stud direction, or use anti-stud connections such as the back of a headlight brick or a Technic brick.

» Some of the simplest and most compact stud-reversal connections have only been made possible with newer parts, such as the 1x1 round brick with hole, which effectively allows you to add a stud anywhere, even on the end of a bar; and a 1x1 round brick with post, which can be inserted into the round brick's hole to create a stable connection.

SNOT bricks allow you to reverse the stud direction, but you need to allow room for the parts required to do so.

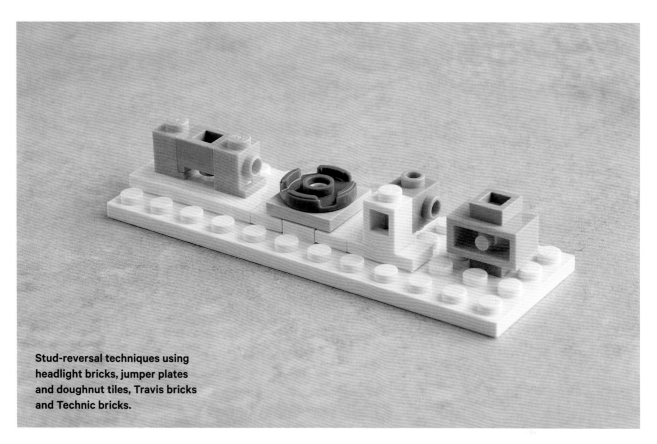

Stud-reversal techniques using
headlight bricks, jumper plates
and doughnut tiles, Travis bricks
and Technic bricks.

Stud reversal in limited
space using retired thin
lampholder plates and
finger-hinge parts.

SMALL STEPS

t's possible to use jumper plates (see page 94) to create even smaller SNOT steps: a quarter of a LEGO plate, to be precise. This slight change of depth can help create more organic textures or subtle details, but requires some space behind the surface to be able to integrate back into the LEGO grid smoothly.

By alternating jumper plates with regular on-grid plates then adding SNOT bricks and Erling bricks you can create a gradual stepping of shapes for much more subtle and organic shapes.

However, this same quarter-plate distance can rear its ugly head when you don't want it to. If you start using jumper plates to centre things, you can often end up with gaps that seem impossible to fill. The problem is that tiny quarter-plate offset. There are very few parts that can effectively fill that gap: the tops of hinge plates and minifig neck brackets probably come closest, though they can be tricky to incorporate.

The edges of 1x2 panels can also form a near quarter-plate step: using the trapping technique (see it in action in *Brickman's Castle Build*, page 134), they can be staggered to form very finely stepped details. This technique has been officially used in the LEGO Architecture Trafalgar Square set.

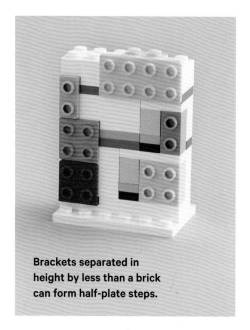

Brackets separated in height by less than a brick can form half-plate steps.

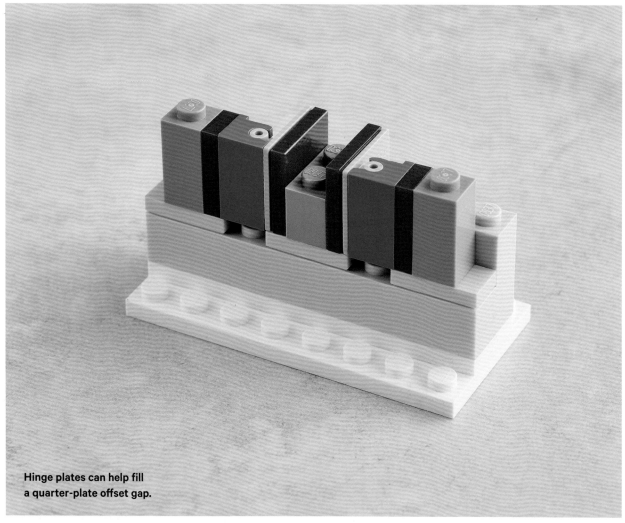

Hinge plates can help fill a quarter-plate offset gap.

OFF THE GRID

The trickiest and most complex form of SNOT comes when you begin to go completely off grid and start to swivel elements and subassemblies using hinges, turntables or ball joints. You may need to use a combination of all of these, along with jumper plates and SNOT bricks, to get the final visible assembly to precisely where you want it to be.

> You may need to use a combination of SNOT elements to get the final visible assembly to where you want it to be.

Here's where you need to really look at off-grid parts such as turntable plates. These are 2x2-stud plates with the studs set in a moveable circular centre – there is a yellow-and-grey one on the far right of the picture opposite – to see how the angles can be created.

When you're trying to create very complex angles or large organic shapes, sometimes one of the best ways is to use Mixels™ ball joints. These allow you to attach a subassembly at just about any angle you want but, because of their size and the clearance required for the joints to work, they can still be tricky to integrate.

Clip-and-bar connections can also allow you to securely swivel SNOT assemblies around a bar at just about any angle but any assembly that uses clips and bars requires extra space within the model.

Ideally all of the sections will attach neatly without gaps or cracks between them, but this simply isn't always possible. The biggest danger in going off grid is creating odd-shaped gaps, which can be impossible to fill using conventional LEGO maths. You can sometimes fill these gaps with small profile elements, such as panels or cheese slopes, but at other times the only way to hide a gap is to literally build over it (see *Disguise*, page 66). If possible, you can extend an on-grid section over the gap, or even build a detail element, such as a pipe or a pot plant, over the top of it to hide it (see *Smoke and mirrors*, page 62).

Turntables placed under an angled assembly are excellent for anchoring them back to the main grid.

TRAPPING

Another useful technique that takes parts off the grid is trapping. This is when you effectively lock a LEGO element or subassembly into a model by building around it so it can't move, even though it's not directly connected.

Trapping can be used in a number of ways, most notably for integrating a complex subassembly that would be impossible or very difficult to attach in the available space. The trick is to ensure the subassembly is prevented from falling out in any direction.

Ideally the subassembly's dimensions will fit the space perfectly, matching the LEGO maths in whichever orientation is appropriate. But realistically this isn't always possible and gaps will appear. If you can't fill them, you can always cover them up with SNOT plates or tiles from the outside.

Plates or tiles can cover edges of trapped mosaic assemblies.

Trapping can also be used to create mosaics of parts that are wedged in together to create a pattern. With this kind of use, you may not need to trap them completely if you keep your build flat, or you could cover the mosaic with transparent panels or windows so that it's still visible, but prevented from falling out (see also *Mosaics*, pages 206–211).

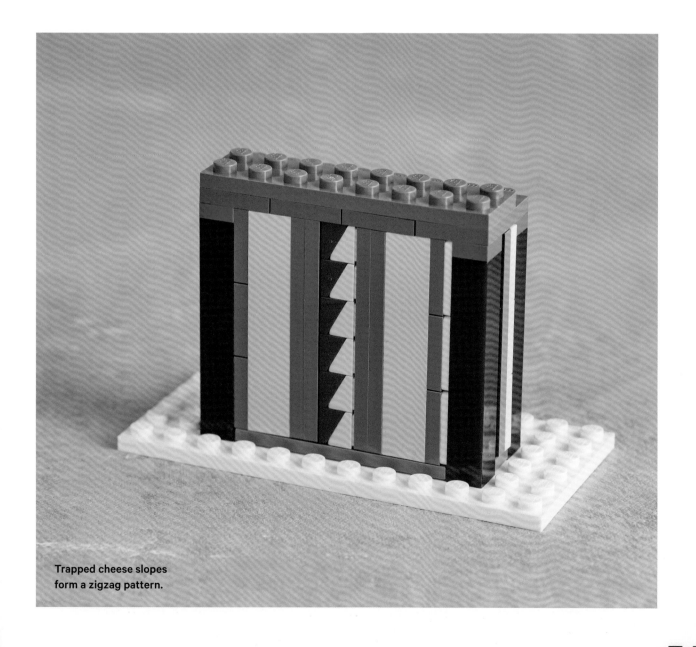

Trapped cheese slopes form a zigzag pattern.

BRICKMAN'S CASTLE BUILD

STUDS NOT ON TOP

The castle uses a number of **SNOT** techniques to great effect. Using **LEGO maths** I was able to turn sections of the build **sideways** and **upside down**. I took walls **off the grid** to allow hexagonal towers to be built. Inserting **SNOT connections** at irregular intervals in the exterior walls made it easy to add decorative textures and finishes.

The balconies on the grey castle turrets use the edges of panels to create **small steps** for the angled stonework. The pictures below show the prototypes (see page 32) I made of the balcony window sections, and at right you can see the sections incorporated into the build.

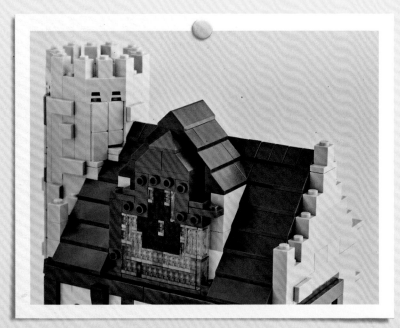

The stained-glass window in the castle keep is built **sideways** as a SNOT mosaic and then **trapped** in place using bricks and tiles.

BRICKMAN'S CASTLE BUILD

Off the grid

The angled walls of the castle bailey are **off the grid**, but SNOT techniques and hinges allow them to be anchored securely.

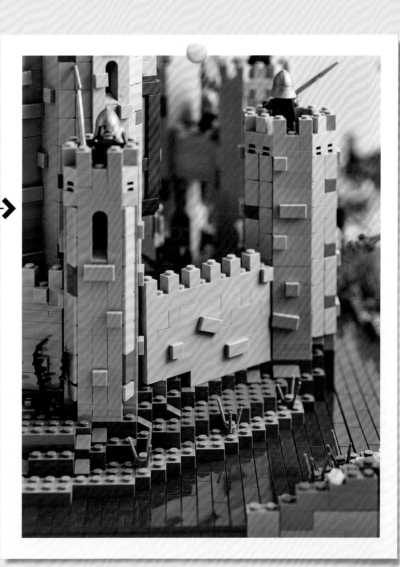

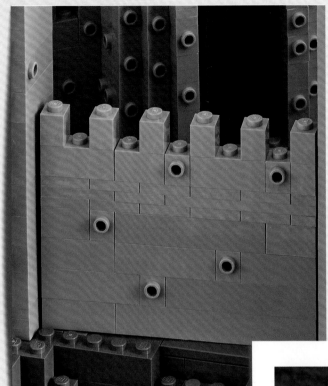

◀◀ Inserting SNOT bricks at random intervals in the castle walls allowed the addition of tiles to create a rough stone texture. You could also use the connections to add ivy and other **detailing** if you like.

Hinges

▶▶ Hinges allow the roof panels of the cowshed to be held at an angle that may not be achievable with straight LEGO System connections. Small gaps in the side walls are filled with **cheese slopes** that sit under the roofline.

BRICKMAN'S CASTLE BUILD

Organic shapes

The billowing clouds of smoke are created by adding round plates to SNOT bricks built into the square column core.

Keep details

The Tudor-style half-timbered upper walls of the keep use red-brown tiles attached to SNOT bricks built into the walls.

Hexagonal towers

Regular SNOT connections down the sides of the towers allow the use of cheese slopes to form the diagonals.

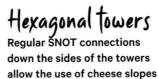

TELLING A STORY

5

If you've watched *LEGO Masters Australia*, you'll know that I'm always going on and on about **STORYTELLING**! It's one of the key features of any great LEGO® model. We all love stories: they **ENTERTAIN**, they **TEACH** and they invite you to **ENGAGE** with a creation. Keep this in mind when building your model – you want to grab the viewer's attention and then hold it as they follow the story.

RELATABILITY

A LEGO model's story can be as simple or complicated as you want it to be: a single moment, or a sequence of events within the same model. But because LEGO models are usually static, the story needs to be clear and easy to follow.

The heart of any good story is a character or situation that the viewer or reader can relate to. You'll see situations you remember, or want to experience, or perhaps really DON'T want to experience. It's the same with LEGO models. Building your model so that it tells an engaging story is an easy way to capture the viewer's interest.

> **For a story to work in a LEGO model you need to be able to show it in a single instant. Start by choosing the most important or impactful moment from a story and work out which characters or models are essential.**

Good vs Bad

One of the simplest ways to build relatability into a model is to use easily recognisable situations, stereotypes or tropes. The simplest of these is 'Good vs Bad': from a young age we're all taught that some behaviours are good and some are bad, and this forms the basis for our ideas of morality.

It's the reason so many LEGO sets are based around teams of heroes and villains, because it's a conflict you can immediately understand and it comes alive in your imagination.

Making your LEGO models relatable is one of the simplest ways to draw people's attention and hold it, but it doesn't have to be high drama with big things at stake, or even a new original story. The best LEGO models come from experience and familiarity, so build things you know well: classic fairy stories, your favourite TV show or something you do or see every day, like playing sport with friends, eating dinner or not wanting to get out of bed and go to work or school.

Relatability is what pulls your audience in to look closer at your model, but to hold their attention you need to tell a story they want to explore.

This freefalling minifig
is held in place with
a transparent piece.

MINIFIGS

LEGO minifigs, with their huge range of facial expressions, costumes and accessories, are the perfect tool for creative storytelling. They can be having fun at a birthday party, crying over losing a toy, running, jumping or falling, or they can be battling monsters in outer space. There are some really clever ways to inject life and movement into minifigs so that they help tell the story of your model.

POSING

Because a LEGO build is static, you usually need to imply movement by posing your model to look as if it's moving. With minifigs this is relatively easy, because they are posable.

For more extreme posing you may need to look at concealing supports that hold the minifig in position: whether it's midair or upside-down. You can use transparent pieces either clipped into hands, or attached to the bottom of a foot or the back of a leg and then attach these to another part of the scenery.

These posing minifigs imply movement.

EXPRESSIONS

>> As human beings, usually the first thing we look at when we see other people is their faces. So it's worth spending time picking, or building, the right faces for the characters in your model. There are hundreds of possible faces for LEGO minifigs, showing a variety of emotions. If you're struggling to come up with a story, sometimes just looking at a minifig's expression can be a great inspiration!

Happy, scheming, sad, scared, angry or cheeky, there's a minifig expression for every story you want to tell.

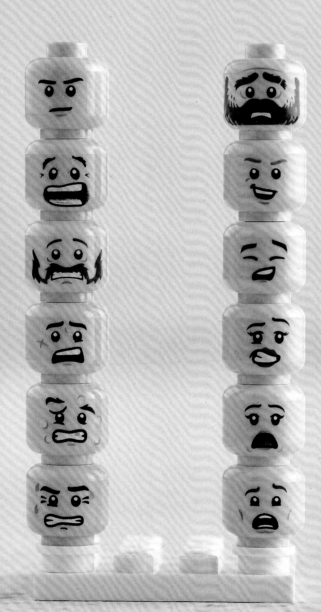

BRICK-BUILT CHARACTERS

I f you're building your characters as larger brick-built figures, then it's important to spend time on their faces for the same reason as choosing the right minifig face. SNOT bricks are great for faces as they allow for more detail in more dimensions, which is important for capturing the complexity and character of a face. Try to include at least three SNOT studs for the eyes and nose and some on the sides of the head for ears or hair, like our brick-built giant opposite. A person's eyebrows and mouth are the biggest indicators of how they're feeling, so they're always a good place to start. N.P.U. (Nice Part Use) can really help: for example, LEGO sausages are great for these facial features as they have an organic curvature and won't overpower other parts of the face.

>> Posing brick-built figures can be a real challenge, as the weight makes balancing them difficult. Giving them a rigid, but light, structural core is important (see **Skill 2: Form and Structure**) and then you can either build them permanently in the pose you need, or include moveable joints so that you can pose them afterwards. If you need to, you can also use hidden supports to help hold them in more extreme poses or carry the weight.

If you want to take your story to the next level (see **Skill 7**) you could even make parts of your model move or light up with LEGO Technic™ and other accessories.

GENRE

Every story can be categorised into a type or 'genre' in some way. Genres help set up what people can expect to happen and guide them to relate to the characters, even if the setting is strange or unbelievable.

You can use genre to assist your LEGO model-making in the same way. Genre gives you an existing palette of ideas to draw from, and gives viewers of your model a recognisable 'in' to draw their attention. Often the genre of your model will be dictated by the subject, but sometimes it can go the other way around, as shown by the Comedy and Horror versions of the same house here.

Some examples of genre include comedy, horror, romance, adventure, sci-fi, fairytale, Western, war, ninja and many more. Genre describes not only the setting of a story but also the types of things that will happen to characters within it. So whether you've built a house where sitcom characters might stand in the garden and exchange wisecracks with their neighbours, or a house that looks like it's full of ghosts and secrets, where anyone who enters will be scared to death, it's genre that begins the story.

Comedy

Horror

MAKE IT OBVIOUS

Using clichés, stereotypes and memes that are common knowledge is an easy way to build situations and jokes that will make people relate to your model. It may also make them want to look for more things they might recognise, thus drawing them further into the model. Clichés are clichés for a reason: they're true! Don't be afraid to make things exaggerated: this makes it easier for people to see and recognise the story. The LEGO Group itself has created an exaggerated, cartoony aesthetic, which works well at a smaller scale.

COMEDY

Comedy and humour are a natural fit for LEGO models and this is probably one of the easiest genres to use. Everyone loves to laugh! Having a character suffer some kind of silly misfortune, such as slipping on a banana peel, getting splashed with paint or running away from a stinky skunk, immediately makes you say to yourself, 'I'm glad that isn't me!' and gives you permission to laugh.

HORROR

Some genres can be trickier, but LEGO minifigs have a lot of scared faces, so suspense or horror can be easily achieved with minifigs.

ROMANCE

Romance is a bit more difficult to depict in a single moment, as it's more contextual. The easiest way to do it is to choose the clichéd moments as visual clues: bringing flowers and chocolates, a proposal, a first date or the first attempt to hold hands.

MASHUPS

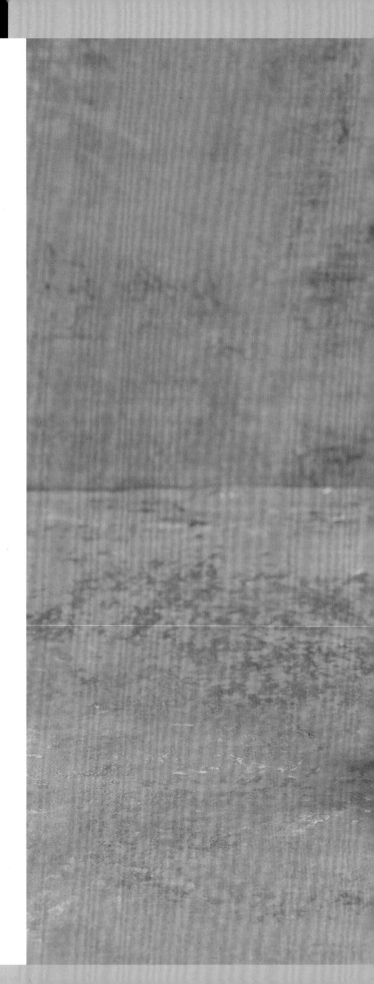

>> You can also use genre in other ways: you can use it to set expectations, but then undermine them with funny or unexpected details to surprise your viewers. Or you can mix genres to create funny combinations of characters and settings.

Creating a mashup of several genres in the same build can open up new avenues of storytelling. Different genres can tell parts of a bigger story in one build. For example, our main character falls in love, but then finds out their love interest is an alien. It might also let you use favourite LEGO pieces or minifigs just for fun.

What story is my sci-fi ninja horror vignette telling you here?

FOCUSING ATTENTION

Part of telling a story well is focusing attention on the key elements of the story. The way you frame your characters within your build is just as important as the characters themselves. The most straightforward way to do this is to simply have the more important parts of your model at the front, so that they're the first thing people see and they're not obscured by other parts of the model. You can also achieve this by putting the important elements in the middle of your build or, if you're building a tall model, placing them higher up.

Aside from prominent positioning, there are other ways to more subtly pull viewers' attention deeper into a model. Here are a few ideas to get you started.

DETAIL

>> Make the focal points either more or less detailed than their surroundings. In this scenario, the plain grey spaceship is surrounded by a lush alien landscape, which contrasts with the smooth lines of the spacecraft.

COLOUR

Make the important aspects of the scene a contrasting colour to the rest of the build. For example, our loving couple is shown in colour among a crowd of monochrome companion minifigs.

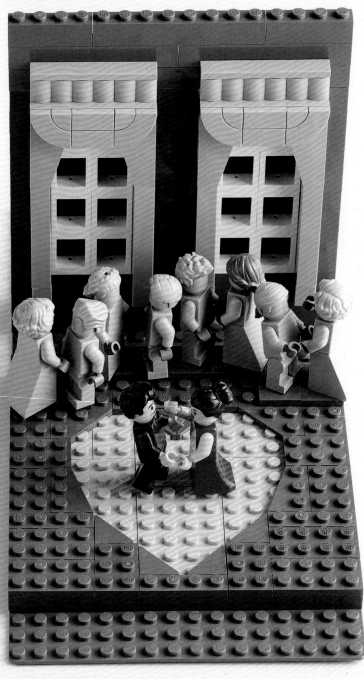

FRAMING

You can also think of the structure of the model as a picture frame surrounding the main action. Place your important story elements first, then literally build the environment around them to give more details of the story.

MAKING A SCENE

Generally speaking, it's best to stick to only one or two moments per model, or you risk overcrowding it, not to mention making the build much harder. If you choose to show multiple moments or scenes from a story within a single model, then using framing or positioning techniques can help separate and make the different moments easier to follow and understand. If the scenes take place at different times, try to build things into their surroundings to show the difference in time.

Summer   **Winter**

A story of growing and growing up.

You can tell more parts of a story in a sequence of smaller builds put together, but make sure the order is easy to follow: left to right and top to bottom is normally the simplest as it follows the same logic as reading in English.

You can also use 'selective compression' (see page 27) to focus attention on different areas of a build. For example, buildings in the distance that are not part of the story can be built smaller and more simply than buildings that are closer to the action, or which the characters interact with. When you are building big things, they don't have to be built at a consistent scale. If a minifig doesn't interact with it, you can make it shorter or smaller. For example, if the action takes place in a garden, you can use just a wall and a window to represent a whole house.

ENVIRONMENTAL STORYTELLING

While it's easy to tell a story by relying on characters and action, it is possible (and challenging) to tell a story just by building an environment that gives all the information you need to follow the storyline. A LEGO model that does not have any minifigs or obvious characters can still tell an interesting tale.

Story is fundamentally about change over time, and having a model imply or show the passage of time and the way it has impacted things can be enough to inspire viewers to create their own story in their heads. Think of visual cues that indicate the passage of time: plants growing over things, cobwebs or things starting to fall apart.

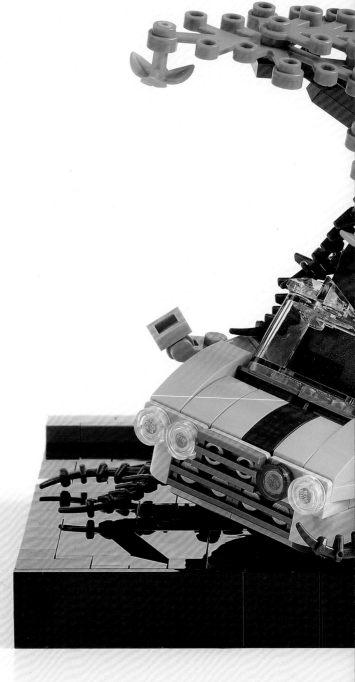

The absence of things you would normally expect to see somewhere tells a story too: you're forced to imagine why something, or someone, is not there. This type of environmental storytelling is used often, for example, in video game design, especially when the user can explore the surroundings for themselves. Using props, details, environmental effects and clues, you can lead the observer to a conclusion that a certain set of events has taken place:

An arrow lies on the ground, surrounded by several loose feathers, next to a tree trunk with large scratches in the bark. A trail of acorns and nuts leads away from the scene, followed by large rabbit footprints which are spaced far apart. The full moon shines down between the branches of the tree.

Even though there is no character in this paragraph, you get a clear idea about what has happened. A story forms from the clues: there are props (arrow, feathers), environmental effects (scratching and footprints) and environmental clues (the trail of nuts and the moonlight). These things all come together to give you a story.

Environmental effects can leave behind evidence that you can see: dragging leaves drag marks; scratching leaves gouges; walking can leave footprints; eating food leaves crumbs; and tyre skid-marks on the road mean somebody had to hit the brakes suddenly. Think about what might have happened in your model, what actions have been performed and what evidence those would have left. You can string an observer along with a few of these and tell a little story about what has happened.

Without a character, this vignette tells the tale of a death and the blossoming of hope after sorrow is over.

You can't see the arrow but our one-eared rabbit is holding a bow and calling for help. Can you fill in the story?

SECONDARY STORIES

While you normally need to choose one or two specific story moments to highlight in your LEGO model, that doesn't mean you can't include other moments from the story or even add a completely new one.

It can be tempting to build lots of fun micro stories into a model, but it's important that they don't overcrowd or overshadow the main story you're trying to tell. Keep the secondary stories or surprise references to a single moment.

EASTER EGGS

One clever thing you can do with models is hide little jokes and references in them. As fun as these are to create, they also serve another purpose – they spark curiosity and, if a viewer recognises a reference, it builds relatability and encourages them to look further into the model.

These hidden jokes are known as 'Easter eggs' because they are a surprise that the viewer has to hunt for, and they make the experience sweeter.

JOKES

In the huge Roman Colosseum model I made many years ago, there were lots of opportunities for jokes. Here, the Emperor is distracting a bear from its fight with a gladiator by offering it a juicy T-bone steak.

REFERENCES

You can transform an ordinary scene by including references to other stories or incidents that are familiar to people – for example, Star Wars® minifigs invading the galley of a jumbo jet.

TELLING TALES

The castle build offered many opportunities to make the story **relatable** on different levels: there are knights and farmers, kings and servants, magic, a dragon and even a giant kitten. **Posing** minifigs to help tell the story and choosing their **expressions** is all part of the fun. The brick-built kitten **character** was another challenge.

While the model is mostly in the historic **genre**, there is enough scope in the story for a **mashup** with some comedy, romance and even horror. **Focusing attention** on the bright red dragon or the wizard framed in the opening of the castle tower was easy to achieve by building their surroundings to draw the eye to them.

The construction of the whole **scene** uses quite a bit of **environmental storytelling** and there are a number of **secondary stories** and **Easter eggs** for you to find throughout the build.

The royal family's traditional dress puts the model firmly in a historical genre.

Drops of magic potion on the brick-built kitten tell the story of how it has grown to such huge proportions compared to the minifig-scale castle.

Expressions

The expression on the minifig farmer's face (above) explains how she feels about her lands being invaded by a fire-breathing dragon (left).

BRICKMAN'S CASTLE BUILD

Easter egg

A treasure trove hidden beneath the roots of a tree is a **secondary story** that could spark a viewer's imagination. Who put it there and why did they hide it? Are the archers defending the hoard or are they ignorant of its location? Does it belong to the dragon or is she trying to steal it?

Secondary story

Everything is going wrong for the resident wizard. An accident with his magic potion is making everything supersized, including his own left arm and hand.

BRICKMAN'S CASTLE BUILD

What a joke!

The wizard spilled his magic potion and that smiling soldier is about to step in something that might give him a BIG surprise.

Environmental storytelling

It's summer: the trees are green and the flowers are blooming. So what's up with this farmer's crop? Have the animals eaten all the grain?

DETAILS

6

If making a **MODEL** is like baking a cake, then the **DETAILS** are the fancy icing and cherry on top. Details are the **FUN BITS**: the little touches here and there that really bring a LEGO® model to life and make it an **IMMERSIVE** experience. A beautifully detailed model takes the observer into the world you have created, **AMAZED** at the completeness of what you have made.

PATTERN AND REPETITION

Well-made details are one of the reasons people make models: to capture something about the subject that's unique, interesting and attractive. Adding detail here and there, like a cake artist with a fine piping nozzle, will round out your model to make it look more realistic.

PATTERN

>> LEGO bricks are excellent for creating patterns. The repeating nature of the pieces means you can make patterns in any direction you like, using studs, SNOT techniques, bricks and plates. Adding pattern to a model using colours and shapes will give it a layer of complexity and interest that can really bring it to life.

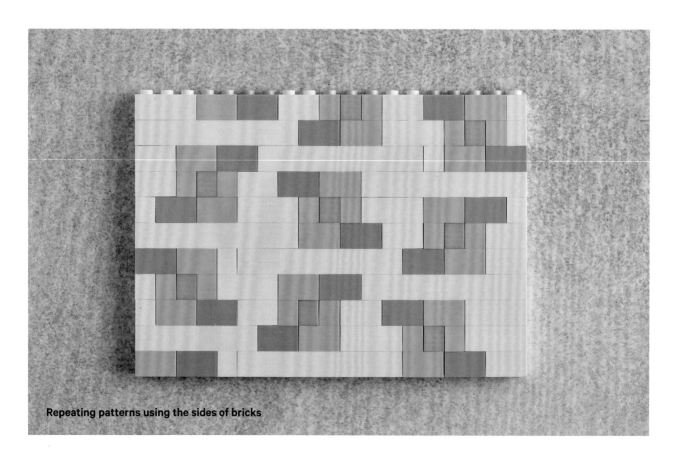

Repeating patterns using the sides of bricks

Repeating patterns using studs

Patterning on the exterior of a model will add complexity. The accurate reproduction of pattern can add to the realism of a build and make the model more convincing.

Do your research and see if you can accurately mimic the pattern of scales on a butterfly's wing. Could a lepidopterist recognise the species you are trying to represent?

ART AND CULTURE

Different societies use recognisable styles of patterning in their art, craft and architecture. Including these in your model can help it better represent a particular culture or location; for example, see the tile patterns on the building façade on the opposite page.

Patterns of the same colours can add consistency in a build, even if the pattern configurations aren't the same throughout. You can suggest variations in texture and form by using large or small pattern variations.

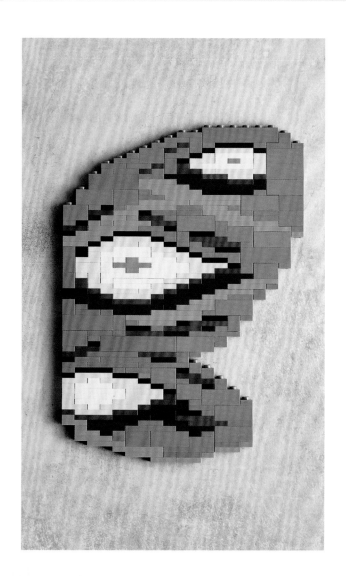

Middle Eastern-style architecture draws on a recognisable range of shapes, colours and patterns.

REPETITION

>> The repetition of similar constructions can help to bring a model together and unify the design. If you make the same section several times in different places on your model, it makes it look consistent, like it's all from the same world.

Using repeated patterns in your build can save time. This can apply to both the construction of the model and the surface decoration. Once you have built one section, copying it exactly to make more of them won't take as long the second or third time. Varying these a little won't take as long either if you don't want things to look too 'samey'.

Creating a tessellating pattern is a great way to make realistic floor tiles. Tessellation is when geometric shapes fit perfectly together, repeating over and over, often in different directions. These patterns can be regular or irregular geometric shapes.

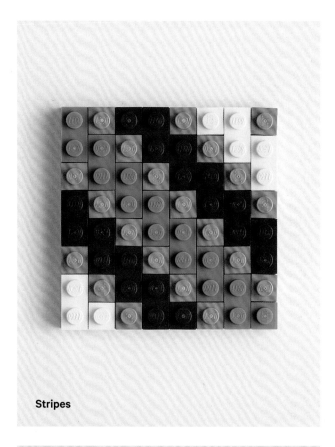

Stripes

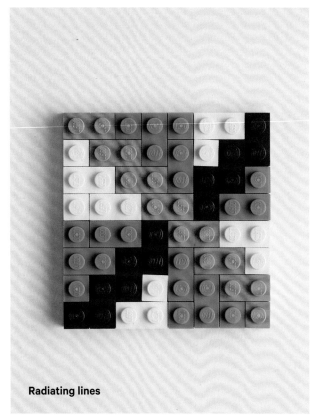

Radiating lines

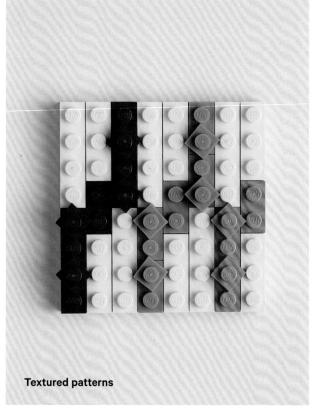

Textured patterns

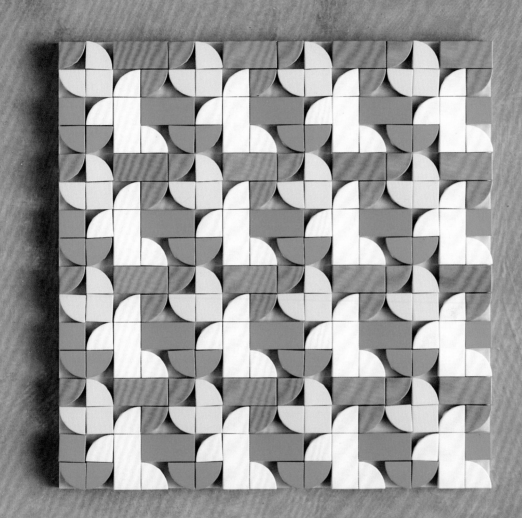

Tessellating tiles

ADDING TEXTURE

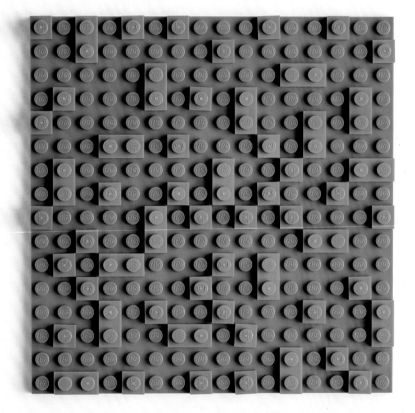

**Layers of studs form
a rough surface.**

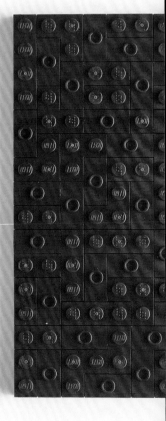

**Jumper plates increase
space between studs.**

To really capture the look of a subject you have to mimic its outward appearance, and this can mean trying to represent many different textures. Sometimes it can be as simple as showing LEGO studs, to mimic the uneven roughness of a surface, or covering the studs with tiles to show smoothness. But often textures are not quite so uniform.

Studs change the look of a surface by adding a kind of visual noise. They have an even pattern that can give the look of uniformity if you need it. But this even patterning can also distract the observer when it's in a place that should have a more natural, random feel to it. This randomisation can be achieved through altering the height of the surface by stacking plates on top of each other, or by varying or interrupting the pattern with jumper plates and tiles.

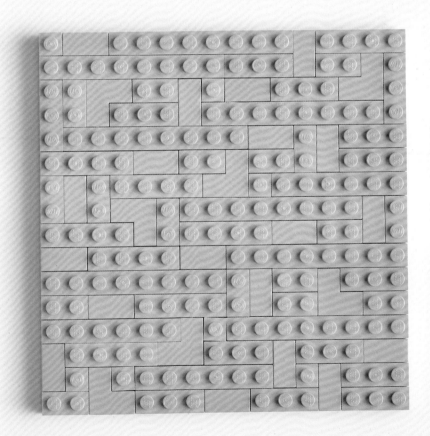

Smooth tiles alternating with studs create variation.

Use the natural gaps between tiles of different shapes to achieve a texture similar to wrinkles.

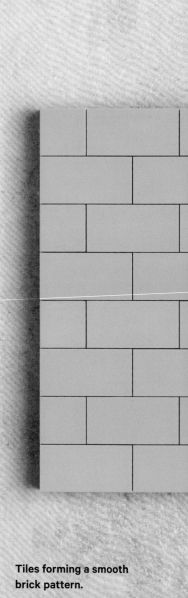

Tiles forming a smooth brick pattern.

Tiles can make something completely smooth, but it's also good to break up the smoothness with some variation. Using only tiles will seem very machine-like and unnatural, so adding some studs or curved edges here and there will add a little bit of visual noise, making it more realistic. Tiles layered with curves and an occasional stud will create a more organic effect.

Using combinations of these techniques just with studs and tiles can give some effective textures, but you can also add other elements to help mimic more complex textures. See the following pages for some examples of the interesting surface effects you can create using tiles, studs, dots, round plates, slopes and wedges.

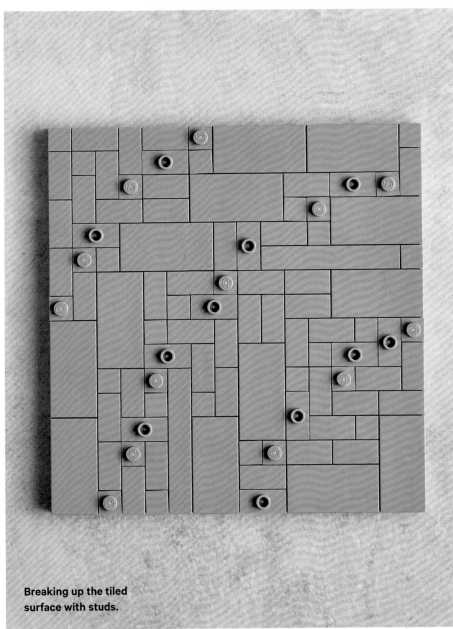

Breaking up the tiled surface with studs.

SURFACE TREATMENTS

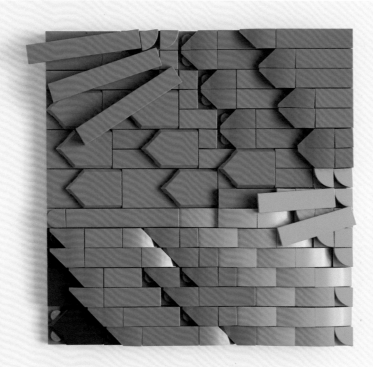

Feathers

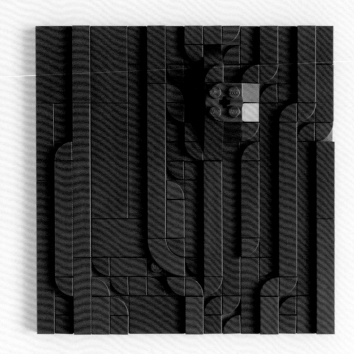

Wood

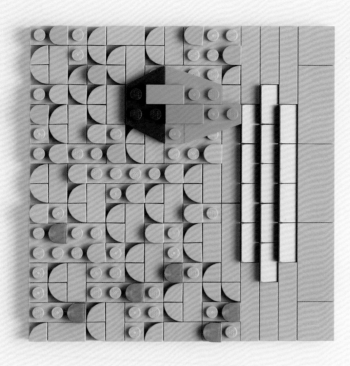

Scales

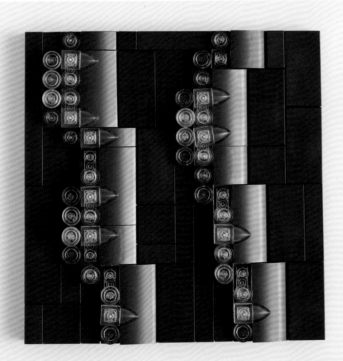

Water

ADDING NATURAL ELEMENTS

When adding elements from nature to your models it's tempting to just make a brown column with some green on top for a tree, or to use a single grey brick for a rock. While this can save a lot of time, it isn't very realistic and, to an observer, could look kind of lazy. Spending time building realistic trees, or detailed rocks, can make all the difference to making an immersive and wonderful world within your model.

Look closely at the natural objects around you and try to work out the basic shapes that form their structures.

It's possible to build natural scenes using just square LEGO bricks, but on the following pages you will find many options and techniques for making more detailed depictions.

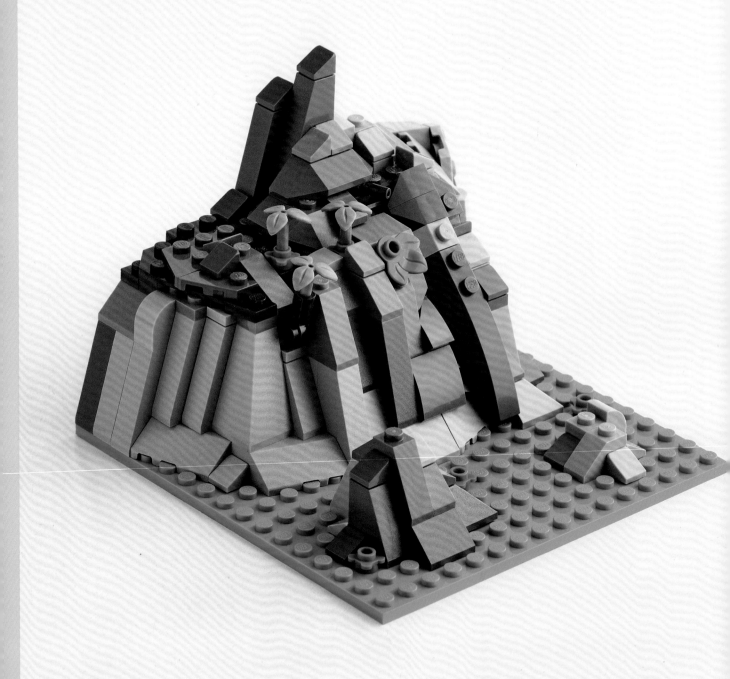

**Small and large
rocky details**

ROCK AND STONE

Single rocks can easily be made using slopes and wedges. A few studs here and there can add a rough texture, and staying away from symmetry will keep them looking realistic and natural; most rocks are non-uniform, asymmetrical shapes. Avoid bright colours (unless you're building an alien planet). Rock faces for cliffs or caves can be mimicked using slopes, curves and wedges, arranged vertically and with larger, interlocking shapes.

Rocks are excellent for covering joins and the edges of natural landscapes. You can pile a bunch of random shaped rocks in corners and along floor/wall joins to soften straight edges and make things look naturally formed.

Stone surfaces for walls can be made in a similar way, but should look flatter and more uniform than rock; the stones have been 'cut', so you can allow sharper angles.

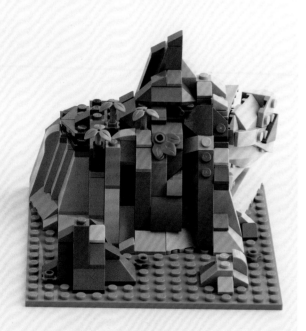

Front view: natural forms

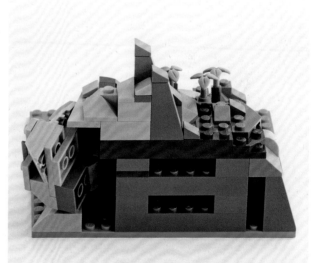

Back view: brick supports

TREES AND PLANTS

If you want to build a realistic LEGO tree, take some time to look at real ones. Trees are not perfectly round columns that come out of the ground like a post. They flare down at the base, hinting at a large underground root system. The branches may not necessarily grow straight out of a central trunk: instead, the trunk may split into two or more branches at various intervals. Branches don't always grow at right angles to their parent either. They usually grow up as much as they grow out, but can also arc over and droop, or grow straight up after a certain distance. It's best to study the kinds of trees you want to build.

Observe the kind of tree you want and note its major features: trunk, roots, bark, branches, foliage, flowers, fruit, shape, height and reach. Start with the trunk shape and then decide how you need to attach branches and whether the trunk has to split. To get the angles of the branches you may need to use connectors: you could use ball joints, clips and bars or hinges.

If your tree subject has branches that split into smaller twigs, you might need to decide how these joints will work as well.

Space your branches at natural intervals, not just extending from the four sides of a brick.

The trunk flares down at the base

Branches grow up and out

Foliage would be difficult to represent if every tiny leaf needed its own piece, but LEGO bars provide an organic base to attach leaf pieces to. By threading the leaf parts onto the bars, the foliage will be stronger and less prone to falling off.

Add leaves and flowers or fruit or whatever your tree subject has in the appropriate season for the model. Observe the colours and shapes in the foliage and replicate them as closely as you can.

There are plenty of LEGO plant pieces that are made in a range of colours, so try the different shapes out to mimic your tree or plant, and match the style of your build.

Foliage pieces in autumn colours

1 Oak

2 Birch

Use variations on these techniques
to make lots of different kinds of trees.

1 An oak tree, for instance, has a thick, rough, unevenly shaped trunk with a large number of big roots. Its branches are quite winding and grow up a little, but out a long way. The foliage tends to be deep green and grow into a dense mushroom shape. It can look like a large piece of broccoli.

2 A birch tree has a thinner, taller trunk, with light-coloured bark and fewer above-ground roots than an oak. Its branches tend to grow out and then up. The foliage is a healthy green and grows at the ends of the branches, so it forms a less dense, long shape at the top of the tree, looking like a brush with a green blob on top.

3 Eucalyptus trees have thin, twisted trunks with bark in varying colours, and their roots are low and flat to the ground. They tend to be tall with branches that grow mostly upwards, but are quite thin and can bend downwards the more they grow out. The foliage is a dull, bluish green and quite sparse, so the canopy is quite thin and looks like little clumps at the top of the tree.

4 Some trees, such as pines or fir trees, have foliage that is so dense that it can be represented as a solid green shape, rather than individual branches and foliage.

5 You can use N.P.U. (Nice Part Use) to represent more unusual foliage, such as green arch bricks used for the drooping leaves of a willow. Or if you need a tropical tree, you can use special LEGO pieces created just for palm trees.

GREEBLES

Greebles (also called 'nurnies') are surface details that look functional but are really just there to make the model more complex and visually interesting. The term was coined by the artists at Industrial Light & Magic to describe the techniques used to make models more believable and realistic.

Greebles can be any small, detailed pieces that make sense on the surface of your model. Try not to overdo it, though, because you might end up with your model looking like a complete mess.

>> If there is anywhere on your model that has a large, flat area lacking in detail you can add greebles to make it more interesting. They don't necessarily have to be technical details like pipes and cables on a spaceship; they can also be organic, like bumps and warts on a monster.

Grills, dots and wedges
used as greebles make
this spaceship look more
high-tech and interesting,
even to an alien Greeble.

PROPS

A nother great way to add detail is to make sure that the characters in your build have all of the right props to go along with what they are doing. Props aren't necessarily just small minifigure accessories; you may also need to build machinery or equipment that suits their activity.

>> For instance, a mechanic might need a large toolbox with a wrench or two, a tyre lever, welding gear and a jack. Props can make the difference between a model with a story that is underdeveloped and one that is more believable.

It's worth doing a little research about your character's job to get an idea of what their props may be, because you are sure to have missed a few. A quick internet search reveals that mechanics might also need things like a toolbox on wheels, an air tank for adjusting tyre pressure, a workbench with more tools and a portable stereo for background music.

If you really want to go into detail, add a tyre balancer, a wheel aligner, a battery analyser, other diagnostic equipment, spare parts boxes, hoists and other lifts, a sandwich-board sign for the shop, a reception desk, a computer, a fridge and more. You don't have to include absolutely everything from a list like this, but some of these things would make your model more realistically detailed. And don't forget, your mechanic also needs a car to work on.

Sometimes you need just enough realistic details to make something believable. Having too few props can make a model feel sparse, while having too many props can make your model seem crowded and claustrophobic.

Every prop you add to a scene tells more of the story.

STORYTELLING WITH PROPS

» Some props can be environmental: things that would exist in the space, but aren't necessarily being used. For example, an alleyway might have bins, boxes, posters, ladders, cats, rats, etc.

Environmental props like this can help add realism to empty areas of the model and let you do some environmental storytelling (see page 162) along the way: using the props to give some extra information about a place or character.

In the vignette opposite, for example, a poster in the alleyway promotes a 'live' keytar concert, but you can see the instrument in one of the bins, along with some pizza boxes and other rubbish. This might give you the idea that somebody's performance was not as successful as they hoped it would be.

Sometimes a single piece like a candle or a cog can inspire a whole build.

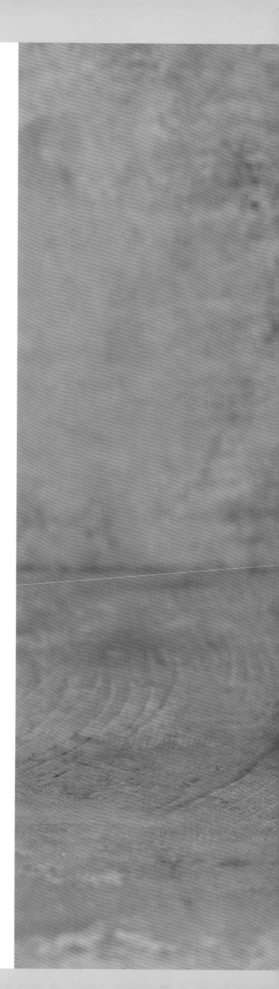

MOSAICS

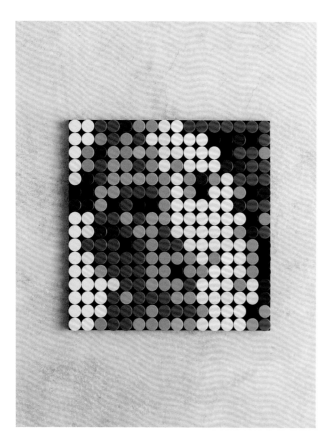

osaics are a simple way to make an image with LEGO parts. Start by drawing a grid over an image. A square grid is best for studs-facing-out LEGO mosaics as on this page: you can decide on the dominant colour in each square of the picture and use that to determine the corresponding LEGO part colour. There are grids to copy on pages 288–293 that can be used for making mosaics (See also *Gridding*, pages 86–89).

A lot of mosaics are created looking at the studs of the LEGO pieces displayed facing out. This is probably the easiest way to create a mosaic because the shapes are squares and the grid that you would use is a regular square grid. You can also use regular image-editing computer programs because the mosaic would be made up of square pixels. Also, in this configuration you can use larger LEGO pieces in the place of groups of 1x1 pieces of the same colour. This can save you having to add a lot of small pieces to your mosaic.

 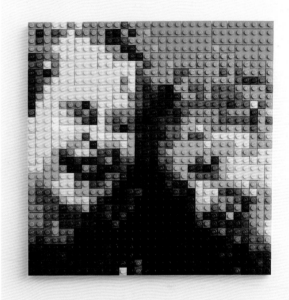

LEGO parts come in a limited number of colours so, when making a LEGO mosaic, you need to restrict the number of colours in your image. Many colours that appear in photographs, for example, are not bright and clear like the colours found in LEGO parts, so you might need to increase the colour saturation in your image. Often colours that are too similar in tone will translate to the same LEGO colour, which means you would lose a lot of your detail. However, you have to be careful when the photograph is of a real human person because if the colour is too saturated, it can appear unnatural when translated into LEGO parts. The two examples above show how different colour choices can affect the overall impression of your mosaic. You don't want to use a lot of tonal colours, as this will make your image appear washed out and the person will look like a zombie, but if you use too much contrast, as on the left, you lose the 'natural' look. Try to strike the right balance between colour and contrast so that your subjects appear natural and the mosaic looks realistic.

You can make mosaics
using the sides of bricks
or plates, as well as with
tiles and studs.

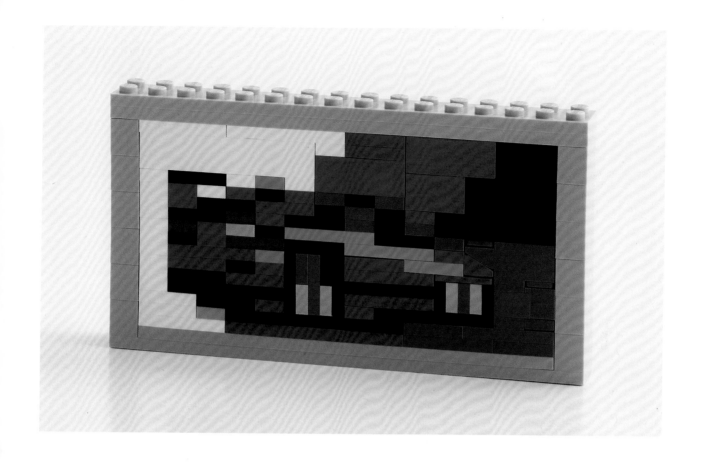

You can also create mosaics using the sides of LEGO bricks and plates, but remember to use a grid that is the same rectangular ratio. A LEGO brick mosaic from the side uses a grid of 1 unit wide to 1.2 units high. A LEGO plate mosaic is on a grid 3.2 units wide to 1 unit high. These are not regular grid ratios; you would have to create these for yourself (or use our sample grids on pages 290–293).

You can easily adjust mosaic colours and shapes if you are unhappy with the results, by removing and replacing parts that look wrong. This may be necessary if your image has been processed by computer, which treats the image as a bunch of pixels rather than a subject, and is unaware of what details are important or unimportant to the image. So don't just take computer output at face value.

Don't forget about your LEGO maths (see page 114) when making an image with plates and bricks. In the space of five horizontally stacked plates that are 2 studs wide, you can rotate the section sideways and it will still fit. This means it's possible to have some sections in your image that run vertically rather than horizontally.

Draw a grid over an image to help work out the placement of your mosaic pieces.

Look at the dominant
colour in each grid
space to work out which
LEGO colour is most
appropriate to use.

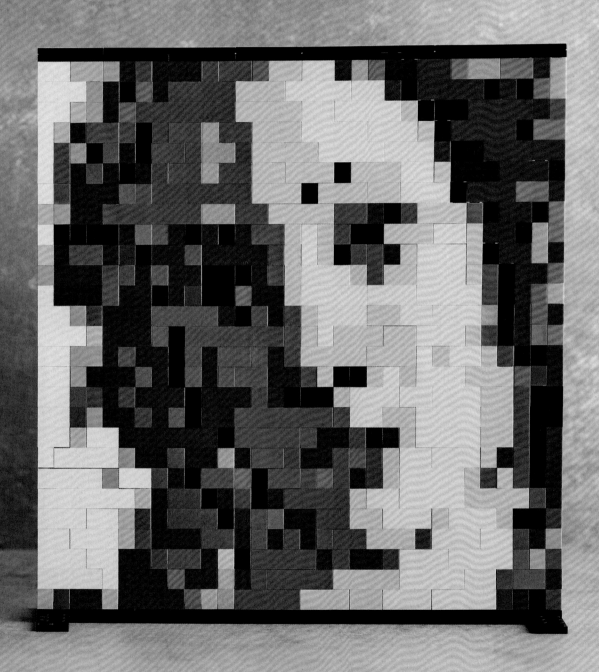

LETTERING

There are a few different ways you can create lettering and attach it to your LEGO models, depending on the theme and structure of your model and what you want the lettering to spell out. You can create brick-built lettering, which is relatively simple and can either be freestanding, as shown here, or attached to your model using SNOT connections. Another option is to create 2-stud high SNOT lettering that is integrated into the build. This is more complex but very effective.

When creating lettering, it's really important that it's as legible as possible to get the message across. You also want it to be strong and sturdy so it stays in place. Finally, you can get creative with fonts and styles to make the lettering an integral part of your storytelling.

Sometimes you literally have to spell out what you want your model to say.

SNOT LETTERS AND NUMBERS

You can use a combination of SNOT bricks and clips to integrate your LEGO lettering into your model. Make sure to leave some room in your design if you plan to have lettering on a certain surface. This is called SNOT lettering and involves a complex construction of plates, tiles, clips, SNOT bricks and brackets to hold it safely in place. (See *Other types of offsetting*, pages 96–97, for an example of SNOT lettering in a build.)

See page 218 for more details on how to make this SNOT letter X.

See page 219 for more details on how to make this SNOT letter D.

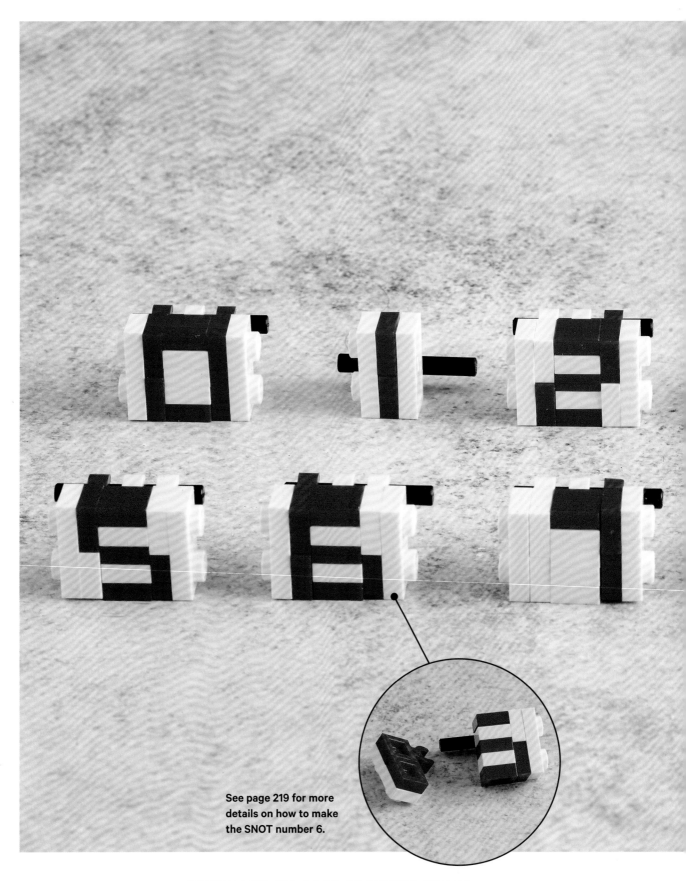

See page 219 for more details on how to make the SNOT number 6.

When making SNOT letters and numbers it is important to remember your LEGO maths (see page 114) and the ratio that five plates fit sideways into the space of two studs. Two bracket-plate widths are the same as one regular plate width. If you have plenty of space to play with when making your SNOT lettering, it will be easier to create, but it's trickier in smaller spaces.

SNOT LETTERING ASSEMBLY

Letters and numbers use just about every type of SNOT connection you can think of.

1. Basic subsections for the letter X ready to assemble. The right side white cheese slopes are attached to two 1x1 plates with clips which are attached to two bars.

2. The smaller 1x2 bracket squeezes in backwards to the larger 2x2 bracket. This does slightly stress the connection, as the 0.1 mm tolerance means the smaller bracket can't sit flush within the large bracket.

3. The final white cheese slope assembly is attached to headlight bricks and two 1x2 rounded-edge plates threaded onto bars, which are then secured to the back of the 1x2 white bracket.

4. The headlight bricks attach to the SNOT brick behind the central 2x2 red bracket assembly to pull the pieces together.

5. The finished letter X. You will need quite a lot of space to incorporate this letter assembly into a build.

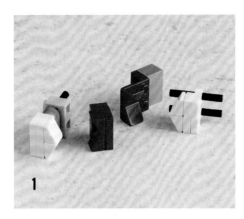

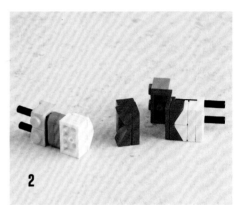

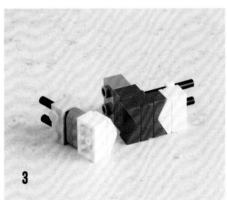

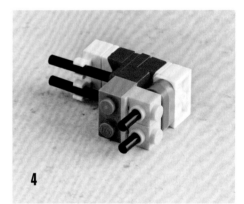

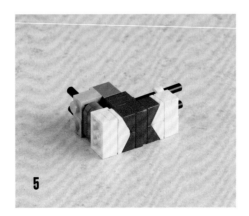

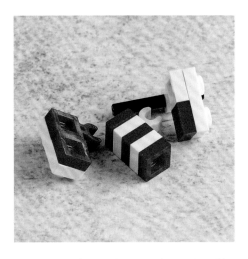

Subsections for number 6 ready to assemble.

Most of these letters and numbers are made using clips that attach to bars.

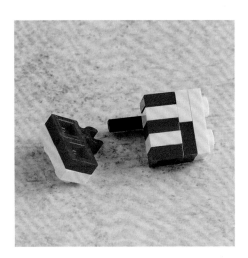

Joining pieces using clips and bars.

Letters such as D might need more trickery, using brackets and cheese slopes as well as clips and bars to get it to work.

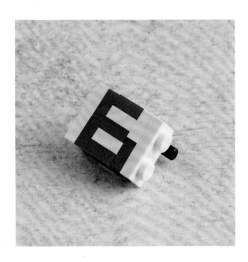

The finished number 6.

FONTS AND STYLES

Experimenting with the font and style of lettering can help set the scene of your model, whether you use freestanding lettering or attach it using SNOT connections, brackets or clips and bars, for example.

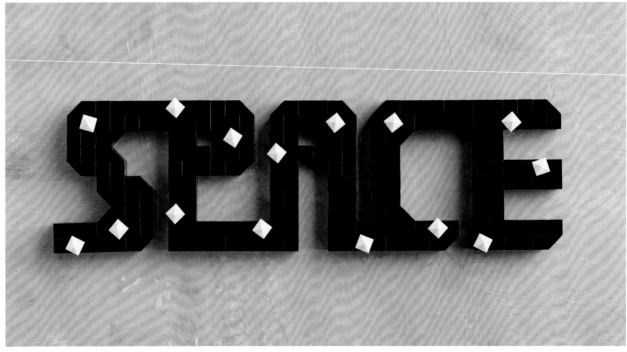

BRICKMAN'S CASTLE BUILD

DETAILS

Adding details to a model is one of my favourite parts of a build. In the castle, I've used **pattern and repetition**, especially with the crenellations along the tower walls. Although the stone walls are mainly the smooth sides of bricks, I added some naturalistic **texture** with **tiles and studs.**

I added **natural elements** such as **trees** and **rocks** in the grounds around the castle, as well as smaller plants, to help set the scene. I also added **props** to help tell the story: there are weapons, a farmer's scythe and a scarecrow, for example.

Crenellations on the barbican are created using pattern and repetition.

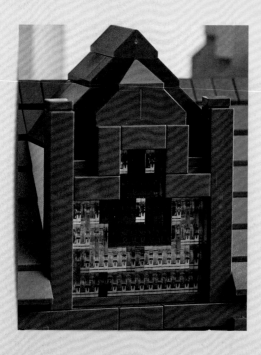

The stained glass window is a sideways plate **mosaic** depicting a red flower growing against a blue sky.

Trees and rocks add interest and realism to the castle grounds.

Props such as the minifig scarecrow help bring the small farm to life and add interest to an otherwise empty area of the model.

BRICKMAN'S CASTLE BUILD

Greebles add texture to the plume of black and grey smoke issuing from the fire in the castle.

Details like the green ivy growing up the castle wall make the build more realistic.

Props for finishing

All the minifig accessories you can find are useful. In the castle, swords are exchanged for buckets of water for the soldiers fighting the fire. A guard dog stands by while the soldiers outside raise their spears in defence against the dragon.

BRICKMAN'S CASTLE BUILD

Texture

The castle walls are kept largely stud-free
to contrast with the studded 'natural'
textures of the surrounding landscape.
The still water of the moat is represented
by smooth dark green tiles.

Details

The blackened ground beneath the dragon and the shattered and burned castle wall sections are brought to life with the addition of LEGO flame pieces. (See also *Environmental storytelling*, page 162.)

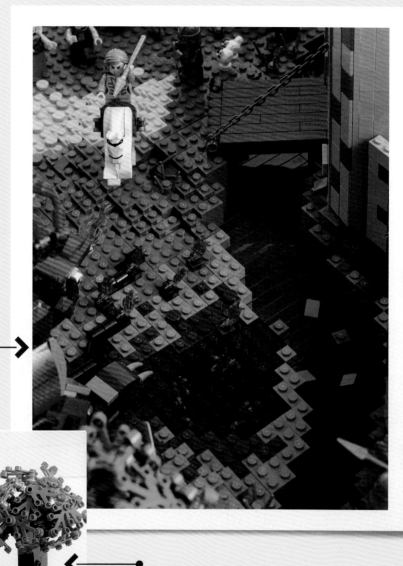

Trees

The types of trees around the castle locate it in a recognisable temperate environment and the variety of building techniques adds visual interest.

THE NEXT LEVEL

7

When are you **FINISHED**? There's a fine line between too much detail covering a LEGO® build, and making sure that there's enough to be **ENGAGING**. One thing that's always sure to be a winner is taking your model to the **NEXT LEVEL**. A well-made model that has extra elements that **SURPRISE** and **DELIGHT** the observer is awesome, and you'll be proud to photograph and **SHARE** it or put it on display.

PLAY FEATURES

When making a model it's always worth doing something 'above and beyond' to really make your build unique and different. Whether it's a secret chamber, an Easter egg (see page 166), some mechanical animation or another special function, adding an element of play or opportunity for interaction is a great way to encourage your viewers to engage with the model.

Adding an action feature that can be initiated by the observer, such as a trigger to make a wall collapse, is a good way to add enjoyment to the viewing experience. Incorporating this in your design beforehand allows you to prepare for the mechanisms you might need to build into the model.

Something observers often enjoy is finding out that a beautiful model of a building has an easily removable wall that allows you to see the detailed interior. Removable walls are quite simply done with tiles at the base of the section and a sturdy self-contained wall piece, plus an exterior feature that can act as a handle. You could even make the wall on hinges so it opens like a door while it stays attached.

A similar technique can be used for a collapsible wall to mimic an explosion or an accident. Create several pieces that slot together to make a wall that appears solid, but will break easily into pieces. To aid this illusion, make the hole in the wall uneven so it looks chaotic. Explosions or crashes are also great opportunities to build interactive mechanisms into your LEGO model. This mechanism could be a switch or brick in the model that viewers can push to trigger a mechanism to push these pieces apart. There are a number of LEGO pieces that can be used to fire something at the inside of the collapsible wall, making the sections fly outwards like an explosion. If you don't have these, you can also create a simple block from bricks that can slide backwards and forwards on a track of tiles. Viewers can then push the block forward from the back, hitting the collapsible wall from behind and making it fall apart.

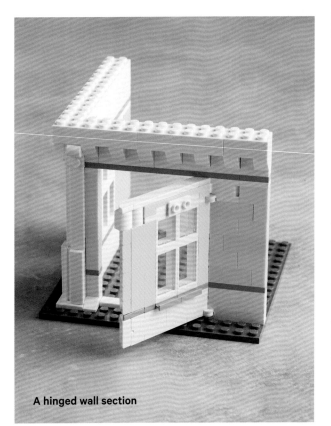

A hinged wall section

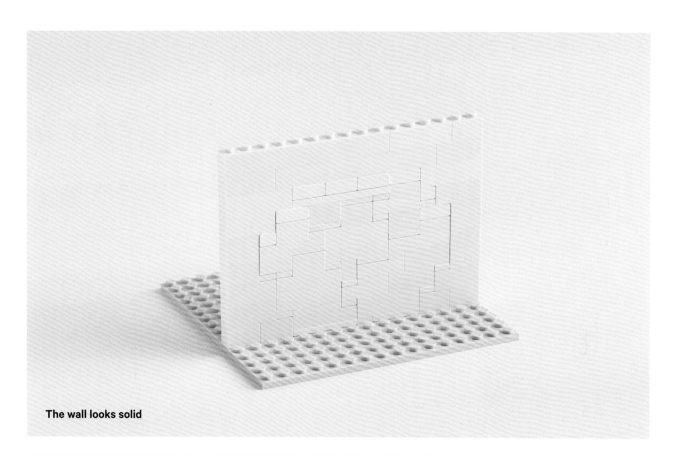

The wall looks solid

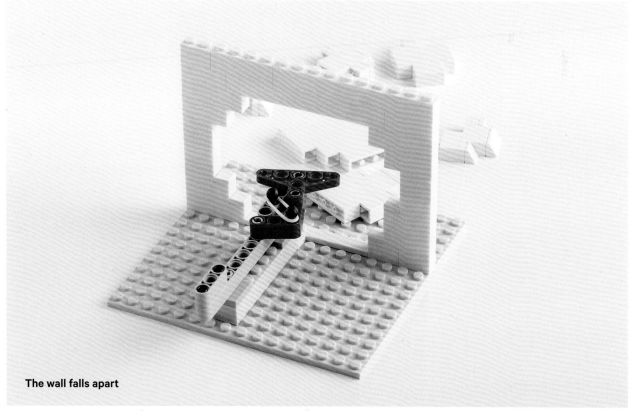

The wall falls apart

231

Another fun feature is building in a secret door. This is a trope from haunted mansion stories and old movies: a secret door leads to a hidden room and inside is something incredible. Hinge pieces make it quite easy to make a hidden door: just allow the pieces enough room to swing freely.

**Who is behind the secret door
in the library of this old house?
Someone is about to find out.**

Alternatively, use a LEGO turntable piece to create a rotating section of wall – another trope from old movies. Set a turntable into a tiled floor and make a double-sided wall. Make both sides the same, but with one important difference.

Perhaps the intruder will come in through the revolving fireplace. Watch out!

Similar things can be done with trapdoors, hidden spooks, or any kind of feature that moves in a simple way. If you prefer not to touch the feature directly, you can add devices that can be triggered remotely to animate these things and add an element of surprise. Place a switch or control where it is camouflaged or difficult to see; for example, behind a wall.

JOINTS AND POSEABILITY

A useful feature in brick-built characters or creature models is incorporating joints of different types, giving you the ability to pose them in various ways. Making a model in a fixed pose can look fantastic, but being able to change and rearrange it as you please will definitely add to its usefulness.

1 Combining a clip and a bar at a join in the model gives a good bending connection. These are excellent for things like wingtips, knees or elbows that really only bend in one particular direction.

2 Ball joints are excellent for dynamic poses as they don't rely on strict angles and can be pivoted in more than a single direction. Using a ball joint for a neck connection allows a creature's head to be angled up, down and sideways, all at the same time.

3 Hinges are also good for knees or elbows, as they do a similar job to clip-and-bar joints, bending only in one direction. With both brick and plate hinges available, you have several options. You'll need to balance the number of connections with the amount of sturdiness you need. Small figures might only need single connections, while larger models will need more to hold heavier sections in place.

4 Don't forget to build around the joints to hide the connections, so that your characters look more natural, but be careful not to obstruct any movement.

1 Clip and bar joints for wingtips.

2 Ball joint for a neck.

3 Hinges for elbows.

4 Build around joints to hide them.

TECHNIC IN MOTION

Using LEGO Technic™ pieces allows you to make all kinds of different mechanisms. You can make things spin, go in and out, open and close, flap, light up, or almost any action you please.

Gears and cogs can transmit rotational motion from one place to another. The speed and direction of the rotation can be changed using different combinations of gears. This rotating motion can be transformed into linear movement using piston assemblies to push or pull things.

These mechanisms can be powered by LEGO motors or hand-driven cranks and can be as simple or complex as you need.

Turn a handle to create rotating motion.

A simple hinge mechanism.

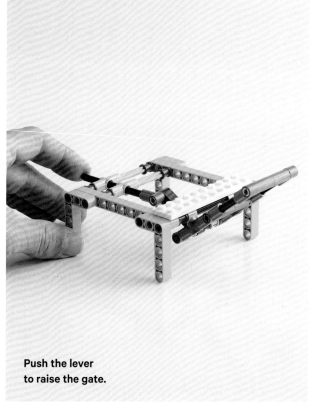

Push the lever to raise the gate.

Attaching legs to wheels gives a range of forward and up-and-down motion.

Repeated motion will make it walk.

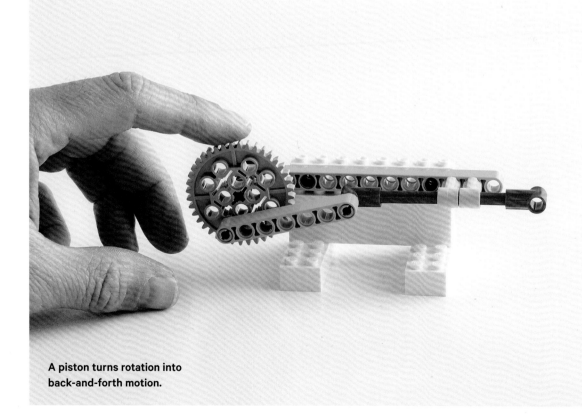

A piston turns rotation into back-and-forth motion.

GEAR TRAIN

>> A false floor conceals complex mechanisms that create multiple types of motion with just one turning handle. In this pizza parlour, the chef removes a pizza from the oven and turns to place it in the display cabinet using a piston. The rollerskating waiter careens back and forth across the floor as a cog turns a rotating track, while the diners take turns helping themselves to pizza at their table with an up-and-down motion. Known as a 'gear train', this kind of mechanism can bring your whole LEGO scene or single model to life with multiple different types of movement from just one turn of the crank. A similar technique is a gear that runs a chain, where notches on the chain trigger the animations.

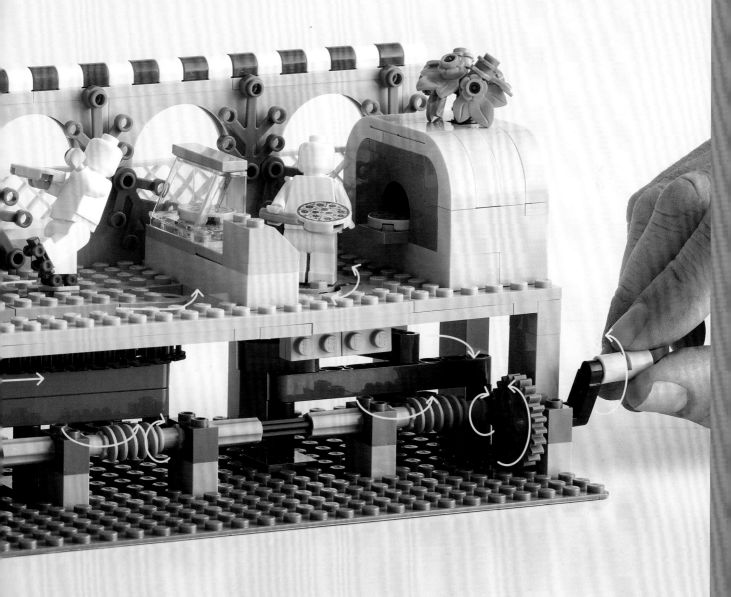

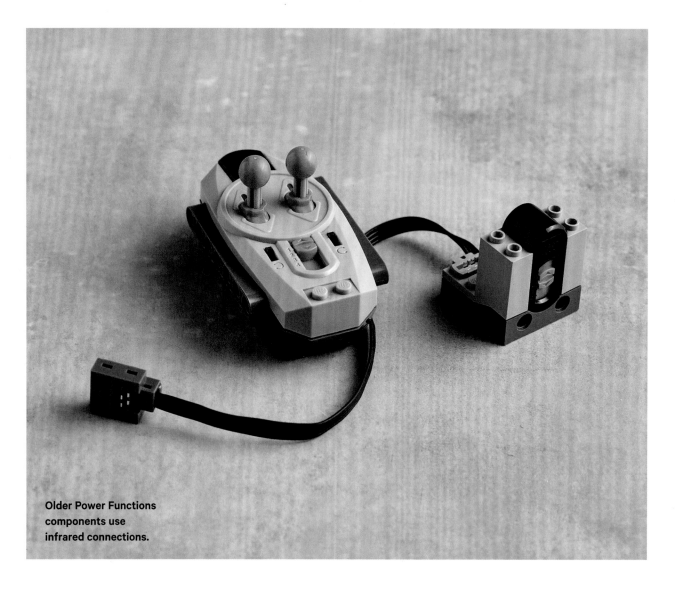

**Older Power Functions
components use
infrared connections.**

POWER

Small motors that can be connected to LEGO models enable many different types of action. With the appropriate structures, a motor can make parts of the model move, or drive the whole model (providing it has wheels or tracks). A motor can also power shutters to open and close, allowing you to light up or darken parts of the model at the flick of a switch.

You can use one of the many different types of motor that the LEGO Group has produced over the years to add mechanised movement to your creations. Whether you want to make a fully remote-controlled vehicle, a simple movement display or a functional machine, there are plenty of options.

There are infrared controls that rely on line-of-sight to control different sections of your build. As long as there is a direct line from the controller to the receiver you can trigger the motion of the motors on and off, changing speed and direction.

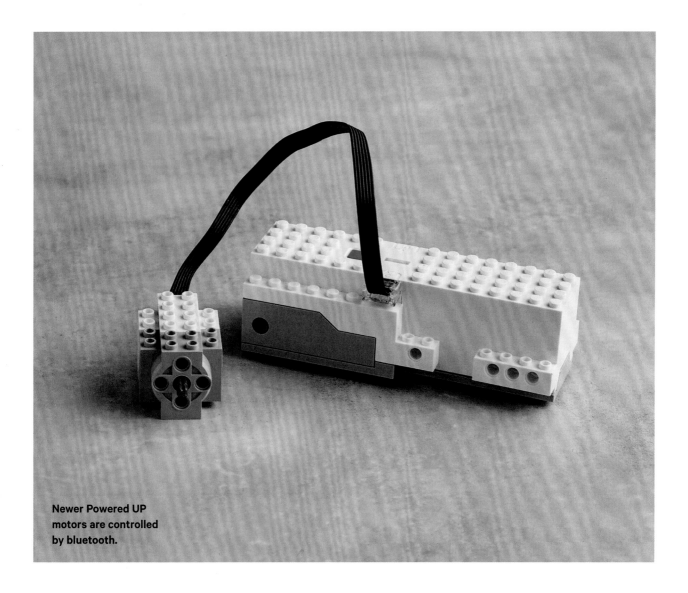

Newer Powered UP motors are controlled by bluetooth.

There are also bluetooth controls that work with mobile devices. From your phone you can control modules that trigger motors, servomechanisms, lights and even sounds. These modules can also be programmed to be autonomous and perform simple tasks with light, sound, obstacles and colour sensors.

Simple mechanisms involve continuous movement or cycles. You can attach minifigs to the mechanism to make it look like they are dancing, or make a dog model that opens its mouth and wags its tail.

More complex mechanisms will have triggers that stop the movement or change its direction at predetermined points, such as a lift that moves up and down a building, stopping at different floors.

Another technique that is useful is a gear train that has several different functions all powered by one motor. Just like in the mechanical gear train on pages 240–241, a line of gears connected to the motor triggers different animations along the line.

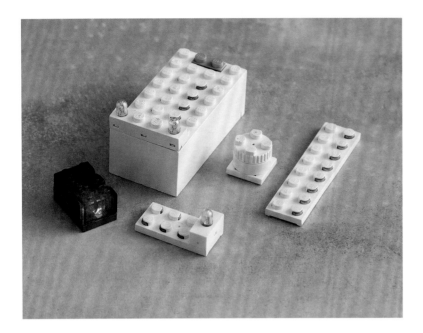

LIGHTS

Lighting up your model from the inside looks great. There are several different LEGO light modules that you can use to do this.

LEGO light bricks come in a few different iterations and mostly require batteries. There are older ones from the 1980s that will flash if you want them to, and ones that you can turn on and off by remote control. One that is still commonly in use today is the push-button brick variety, which works well, although it does tend to go through batteries quite quickly.

If you don't mind using non-branded parts for your models you can buy strings of party lights that run on batteries or power and, with a bit of imagination and hiding of wiring, you can make them suit your build.

There are third-party light kit products, mostly designed for specific LEGO sets, but these can be adapted with a bit of electronic know-how.

If you have the skills, the time and the budget, you could make your own electronics, wiring up LED lights through your entire model.

If wiring and electronics is not your thing, there are new kits that work with electromagnetic induction to light remote LEDs with their own tiny receiver. They work with batteries or power to run a transmitter that is a loop of wire, about the size of a dinner plate, which can be placed either inside or under the model. It emits an alternating magnetic field that powers the lights, which can be placed anywhere in a model, as long as they are within the field. The LEDs come in white, red, blue, yellow, green, magenta and orange, and the transmitter has a limited range. These kits are not widely available, but you can hunt them down on the internet.

> **If you want to brighten up your models, this should be an illuminating section.**

Battery-powered LED
party lights work well.

DOCUMENTING

Once you've added all the bells and whistles to take your build next-level, it's a good idea to document your work so you can refer back to it in the future. If it's going in a display or exhibition, you may want to take pictures so you can show the event organisers what the finished model should look like, in case you're not present when the modules of your build are put back together. Taking good-quality photos of the full model and its featured details can also be used for articles, for your portfolio, for social media and for display purposes.

You can document tricky builds in the form of instructional guides on how to recreate them – photos with descriptive text are the best option. If your model is a complex modular construction, it's good to document step-by-step instructions on how to put the sections together. Believe it or not, it's quite common to forget aspects of your build and how it goes together, so documenting your work as you go is also a good way to remind yourself how you did it.

It's good to keep the documentation in the storage or shipping containers with the model in case of emergency. Even if you plan on disassembling the build, you may still want to refer to aspects of it at a later date.

Write lists and detailed instructions to go with your photographs so you never forget how you built a model or a part.

PHOTOGRAPHY

There's enough to be learned about LEGO photography to fill a whole book, but here are just a few very simple basics.

Clean and tidy the model, making sure that everything is in the right place for the photos. Double check that all the pieces are pushed together. Arrange the model and pay attention to the details, especially if you're taking close-ups, as small imperfections and any misplaced pieces will be blown up large. Get rid of any dust and stray hairs before taking the shots, but don't worry if you spot detritus in the images, as you can use an image editing program on your computer to remove it later.

When photographing the model, take your time: you don't want to rush, then realise something was out of place once you've already packed away. Review your photos as you take them, and zoom in to be sure the right areas are in focus.

You don't need an expensive SLR camera; most phones these days produce great pictures.

Use white cardboard and small household lights to set up your home 'studio' space.

LIGHTING

When photographing your model, it's best to get the level of lighting right so you can see detail in the shadows of the photos: not so much light that the image has bright white patches (hot spots) instead of small highlights, and not so little that there are a lot of black patches instead of detailed shadows. Having the right amount of even light allows you to capture detail in the model, and no amount of editing software can help if the photo is underexposed (too dark) or overexposed (too light).

It's better to have at least two light sources, and you can use white boards (any flat white surface will work) to 'bounce' (reflect) light indirectly towards the shadowed parts of the model.

Soften the sharp shadows of harsh lights by placing a piece of thin white fabric or tracing paper in front of the light. (Be careful to avoid putting things over the light globe itself, as it is very hot and you don't want to start a fire.) If you want to spend a bit of money to set up your home photo studio, you can buy inexpensive softboxes online which soften the light.

A backlight behind the subject, pointed at the rear to lighten the back edge, looks very nice and helps to illuminate details in the shadows. Lightboxes can be good for taking shots with nice, even lighting.

Shooting outside during the day provides good light as the sun and the sky count as different light sources. A cloudless sunny day will produce harsh shadows when the sun is high in the sky, so taking shots in the morning or late afternoon can give even light and colour to your model. Bright but overcast days will give good lighting as the sunlight will be more evenly spread and eliminate harsh shadows.

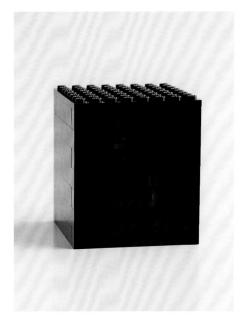

Avoid taking photos with light sources reflecting off shiny LEGO brick surfaces directly into the camera lens: you don't want to see a flaring lightbulb or the shape of a window. Watch out for the reflections of people and other items, too.

Don't lose focus! Always check that what you want people to notice first in your photo is in the sharpest focus.

BACKGROUNDS

Take your photos against a background that has a clean, even colour and is clear of clutter and mess. A light-coloured wall with no patterning or features makes lighting easier.

If you want to take the photo against a more complicated background, try to ensure it is not too busy or distracting from the subject. If you can blur the background (either by using a short depth of field focus in the camera, or image-processing software), this will keep the feel of the environment without too much of the distracting detail.

You might want a picture (such as a landscape) in the background – if so, you can use a computer screen or a TV to display the image. This approach gives nice lighting, realism and depth to the photo and you can control the image on the screen, editing it and adjusting colour and brightness.

Some people use a long roll of paper that hangs down and curves forward underneath the subject, making a nice even, curving backdrop that isolates the model in a single-coloured space. You can set up props and relevant items for the backdrop in this space, but again, don't go overboard and distract from the model.

Another way to take good model photos is to take them in situ, with the model on a stylish modern shelf or table, with a few props designed to enhance the way the model is displayed.

Experiment with different backdrops and techniques to see which you prefer, as different models can look good in different situations.

A clean background makes the model the hero.

If the background is
busy, keep it slightly
out of focus to avoid
distraction.

SHOOTING

There are lots of different techniques to try when taking your photos and it's a good idea to experiment and see what works well and what doesn't. Moving the camera in close and focusing on small details, while letting other parts of the model drop out of focus, will allow you to highlight particular features in their context, as pictured here. Moving the camera further away from the subject and then zooming in will give you less background and a flatter image. Deeper models will seem to compress more and you'll get more of the model in focus.

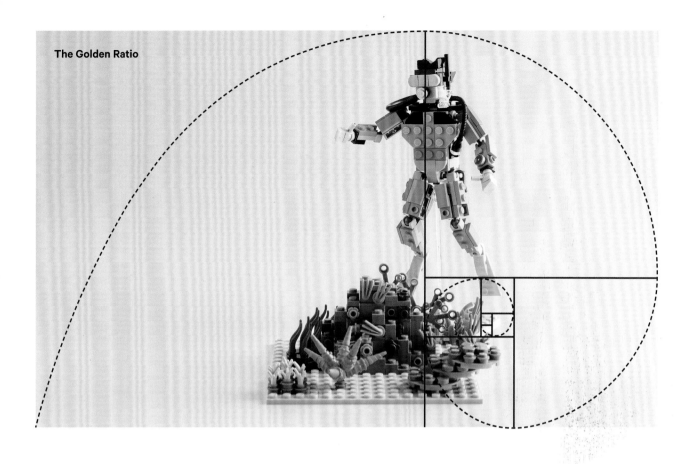

The Golden Ratio

FRAMING AND COMPOSITION

Consider the framing and composition of the shots you are taking – usually photos have more impact when they don't include too much to look at. Try not to crowd the frame; use each photo to feature one thing. If you want to feature two aspects of your model, take two photos. Don't include things in your photos that aren't important.

In art and photography there is a convention called the 'rule of thirds'. Try and picture your image ruled into thirds vertically and horizontally. The four places those imaginary lines intersect are special spots to position important things in the image. For instance, if a character is important, try locating their eyes at one of these spots and the object of their focus at another

of the intersections. You may need to rotate the model or reposition the lights and camera to get this right, but it tends to be worth the effort.

Another good way to arrange compositions is to use the Golden Ratio (an internet search will show you how this mathematical equation works). The Golden Ratio traces out a pleasing visual spiral that works its way from the middle of one part of an image up and around to the other. Placing the subject of your photo at the centre of the spiral and having other elements trace out the arms produces quite an engaging image that pulls you into the subject. It takes a little effort, but the result is worth it.

SOCIAL MEDIA

If you're planning to share your images on social media, you should consider the format that is allowed. Some photos look better in either portrait or landscape formats – especially on phones – and some social media formats are square. These factors will change your composition. Be aware of the destination of the image as you take it so you can be prepared to crop it. For example, the portrait image of the spider's lair below has enough space at the top and bottom to be cropped square.

You should take multiple shots to highlight detailed areas – especially if the model is quite large – as the resolution on handheld devices is not clear enough to show all of the intricacies of your work. If you include zoomed-in photos of the more interesting features, it will be more useful for your followers.

You can use image editing programs to enhance colours and add special effects – backgrounds, lightning, speed blurs or text – to enhance your image. Try not to overdo it, as this might obscure what you are trying to show.

BRICKMAN'S CASTLE BUILD

BRINGING IT TO LIFE

This has got to be one of the most satisfying parts of any build; adding the elements of action and play that bring it to life and really take it to the next level.

I built a number of **play features** into my castle model. A **collapsing** wall, a drawbridge that **opens and closes**, and a **poseable** flying dragon with multiple **joints and hinges** give the observer plenty of things to see and interact with.

I also included a **mechanism** to turn on **lights** and make the transparent orange and yellow bricks inside the castle glow, in an illusion of flickering flames.

A simple press of a lever causes the tower wall to fall.

This drawbridge mechanism is an important action feature of the castle.

The poseable dragon model is a great object to play with.

BRICKMAN'S CASTLE BUILD

Lights

Transparent LEGO pieces in orangey colours
create the illusion of a burning building when
lit up from behind. I used inexpensive LED
fairy lights with a battery pack that was
hidden inside the castle.

Eerie effects

Of course the fire looks more scary and realistic when the rest of the castle is in darkness. This kind of dynamic is all part of the playability of the model.

BRICKMAN'S CASTLE BUILD

PHOTOGRAPHY

>> With the camera close to the subject, zooming out takes a wide-angle photo with more **background** and deeper focus. This can make a model seem larger and more spacious. Zooming in and focusing on one particular feature creates a more specific view of the subject. If you're posting pics on **social media**, remember that close-ups can help people focus on details.

Focusing on the portcullis and letting the foreground and background blur creates an intimate viewpoint.

Taking a photo from up high, looking down at an angle (above left), will make the model look small and compact, while taking a photo from a low angle looking up and across (above right) can make it look taller, bigger and more spacious.

>> When **shooting** photos that feature minifigures be sure to take them at the eyeline or similar height to the figures, as you want to capture the faces and expressions. This helps the viewer to connect with them more personally. A photo that is taken from too high a viewpoint makes the minifig look too small and this disconnects the viewer from them.

BRICKMAN'S CASTLE BUILD

Framing and composition

If you need to, you can remove sections of the model so that you get the angle or the shot you need. Depending on your lighting, you may also need to remove sections to make sure shadows don't ruin a photo.

Documenting

Take photographs of your model as you complete different stages to remind yourself how it was built.

Home studio
You don't need a professional photography setup. White cardboard and inexpensive lights will help you take great shots.

MY FINISHED CASTLE BUILD

Here's the finished castle build; I'm pretty pleased with how it's turned out. If you want to take a closer look and zoom in on particular details, you can download a pdf at **thebrickman.com/brickman-better-builds-downloads**.

I hope the information in this book has given you some useful new skills and inspired you to tackle your own imaginative build, big or small. I'd love to see how you go; share your creations on social media using the hashtag **#brickmansbetterbuilds**.

LEGO LOGISTICS

've dropped and broken my fair share of LEGO® models in my time, the worst being a giant Eiffel Tower: more than three weeks' worth of work, all gone in a heartbeat! This section contains all my best tips for moving and storing my LEGO collection and models. There's also advice on healthy building practice: ways to keep comfortable to avoid injury and how to make sure your working environment is suitable for the activities associated with planning, testing and creating your models.

Build regular breaks into your schedule.

HEALTHY BUILDING PRACTICE

» Choose a comfortable, supportive chair to sit on and try to maintain correct posture while seated or standing.
» Don't build for too long with the level of your building at shoulder height or above, to prevent muscle strain.
» Don't lean out or stretch up for more than short periods as this will strain your back.
» If you are standing for a long time on a hard floor, invest in an anti-fatigue mat that cushions your feet, and stops you getting tired and sore feet, legs and back. If you have to kneel, use a pad to kneel on, and don't do it for very long.
» If you can find a sturdy, adjustable height table, lift or lower the model to a comfortable height for you: don't try to contort yourself into odd positions.
» If you are building something large that will need lifting once it is complete, build it on a board, so that when you have to lift it later, the board will provide a safer lifting platform.
» If your model is tall, split it up into smaller, lighter modular pieces that you can connect together later.
» If your shoulders, neck and back get sore, have a break and review your building posture.
» Take regular breaks from building. Do some body stretches or hand stretches, get a drink of water, sit for a few minutes in the sun or go for a walk.

LIFTING AND CARRYING

When lifting bigger LEGO models, you should wear padded gloves as the LEGO edges can be sharp and dig into your fingers. Models that don't seem too heavy to begin with will feel much heavier the longer you carry them and can really strain your hands. If possible, slide a piece of wood beneath the model, or build it on a board, and use this to carry it and help support all the bricks at the bottom.

Never carry or transport a model with its stud connections sideways, as it's too easy to cause a split between layers, with gravity pulling down on the two different ends. Always transport a model with the studs facing upwards – even if it's not built that way – to make gravity work at keeping your model together instead of tearing it apart.

Make sure the path between the load and its destination is clear of obstacles and tripping hazards.

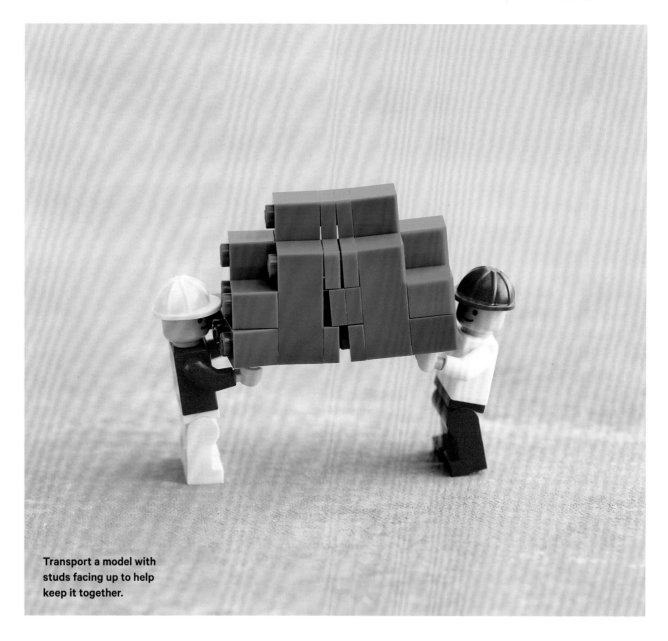

Transport a model with studs facing up to help keep it together.

Separate modules make transporting and storing complex builds easier.

SAFE LIFTING PRACTICE

1 Keep your feet apart at shoulder width to support the weight and keep balance.

2 Squat with your knees bent, down to the level of the load OR put one knee on the ground and the other leg out in front, bent, with the foot flat on the floor.

3 Maintain a good posture: with your back straight, look straight ahead, chest out, shoulders back, keeping the natural curve of your lower back.

4 Lift by straightening your hips and knees slowly, without twisting in any direction. If you find the load is too heavy, set it down immediately and ask for help.

Don't be afraid to ask for help if you can't manage the job safely by yourself. Here's Luke to help us out.

5 Keep the load close to you at about belly button height: do not try to lift anything that is higher than shoulder height and do not bend at the waist or stretch out to the load.

6 Move slowly, taking small steps and turning using your feet. Do not twist your body: keep your shoulders and hips in line.

7 Do not try to hoist the load up above your shoulder height. Ask someone to help you lift it up high.

8 To set the load down, bend your knees and hips, squatting down and keeping your back straight.

If you don't have a supporting board, lift your models from the bottom edge close to any structural support sections and, if you can, steady it by holding the main structure. Don't lift it by holding the outside of the LEGO parts or any attachments that aren't connected well. Try not to lift from too high up on the model as the lower section may pull away from the top section. Place it on a trolley, if you have one, and make sure it is well supported when you tip the trolley.

If a model is too big to be lifted by two people you should consider using a dolly: a platform on wheels. Have two or more people lift the model straight up, then get another person to slide the dolly underneath. Use two people to wheel it to where it needs to go.

TRANSPORT

>> You may need to pack models for moving or shipping. If you are going to display your model at an exhibition or convention, you'll need to pack it into a box or wooden crate to move long distances safely. Cardboard is the cheaper option, but is more prone to damage. Keeping the container the correct way up with the studs facing upwards will help the model remain intact, and adding some tape that says 'FRAGILE' should help to protect it during shipping.

Remove any long and thin, fragile, loose, or swinging pieces so they don't break, rattle or flap about, then pop these in a resealable plastic bag, which you can stow in the container with packing material around it. Long-distance travel will cause vibrations in the model and may shake sections apart – you should first loosely bag each section in case pieces do fall off, so they won't get lost. Tightly wrap the bagged sections in packing material so nothing can move too far or split apart.

WRAP IT UP

Loose pieces in a container tend to rattle about, crashing into other parts and loosening them as well. You want to minimise how much the model can come apart, as even a small number of loose pieces can bump into the rest and cause the model to break up. The worst-case scenario of bad packing is when you open the container at the other end and you find a box of loose pieces and no model.

Wrapping your model in sturdy, stretchy plastic wrap will prevent it splitting apart, but be careful not to put too much strain on the model. The stretchy film can be re-used later if need be.

Place a foam rubber pad in the bottom of the box to help minimise movement of the model during shipping. It's better to use a foam that's stiff and springy for large models so it doesn't get squashed, but you can use foam that's rubbery and softer for smaller models. You can pick up foam rubber cut to size from hardware or specialist stores. Alternatively, bubble wrap or packing peanuts, which you can get from office supply stores or post offices, are both good as well.

MODULARITY

<< It's helpful to make your builds modular for ease of construction, to save space and to make them lighter. Separate sections of LEGO models are easier to lift, carry, ship and store (see **Skill 2: Form and Structure** for more about modular building).

SORTING AND STORAGE

I f you are serious about building large, complex models, you should be sure to sort out the LEGO parts you are intending to build with. Knowing where to find the exact piece that you need for a model can save you a lot of time. Set up a sorting system to arrange all the pieces; once you have it up and running, adding and sorting new pieces won't be a problem.

STORAGE OPTIONS

There are lots of storage options at different prices for all kinds of budgets. Shop around and see what is best for you and what is affordable. Craft and hobby stores supply boxes for beads, jewellery and other tiny pieces. Some have shelving units with little trays. Fishing tackle boxes are also good for smaller bits and pieces, while hardware stores have storage drawers for screws and nails that are great for slightly bigger pieces. You may find good storage containers and cabinets with various-sized drawers at department stores and office supplies stores. A range of different sizes is good, because small pieces in a large container may get lost, while you don't really want larger pieces of the same kind spread over several containers.

Resealable plastic bags can also be pretty handy for sorting and storage. You can buy a variety of different sizes from supermarkets and hobby shops. Be sure to roll out any of the extra air from the bag before closing, as you probably don't want to be storing bags of air.

A collection of washed and degreased takeaway food containers is also handy for holding and sorting pieces. If you want to use these for storage, make sure they have their lids.

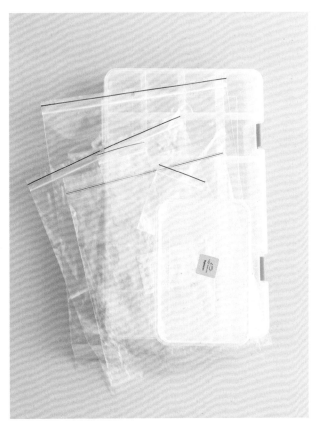

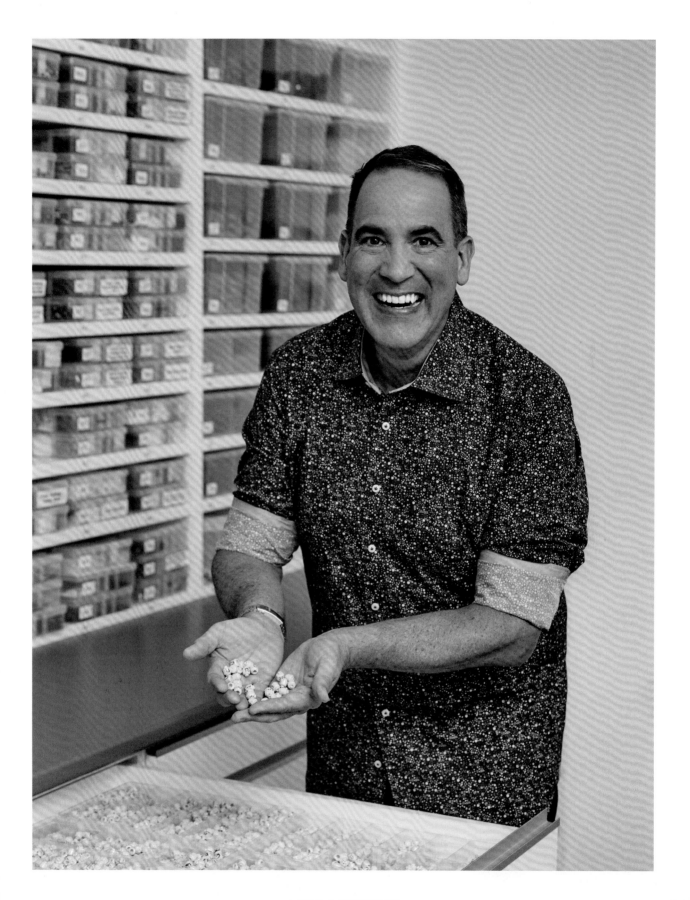

LEGO LOGISTICS

SORTING METHODS

Once you have enough storage for your LEGO parts, you should decide how you want to sort them. It needs to be a logical, well-defined system so that you won't get confused about where pieces should be.

The way you like to build dictates your organisation too. You can prioritise the storage of certain pieces or types of pieces to be more accessible if it's something you use more often; for example, if you like to include lots of trees and plants in your models, make sure you keep those pieces together and can access them easily. It's worth thinking about what your most commonly used pieces are and making those easy to get to, while the stuff you use the least is tucked away.

There are several ways you may decide to sort the pieces and there are pros and cons to each.

SORTING BY COLOUR

➤➤ Sorting by colour is nice and simple: all pieces of a matching colour in the same container. If you need a blue piece, it's in the blue container. You may break it up into sizes – large pieces and small pieces – but they would still be all the different pieces together. The downside of this system is that it can be hard to identify the single piece you are looking for in a sea of the same colour.

SORTING BY ELEMENT

➤➤ The optimum way of sorting LEGO parts is each piece in each colour separately stored. This makes it easier to find what you are looking for, but it tends to take up a lot of room. Most people don't have an infinite amount of room to store LEGO parts like this, so you will need to decide how to group your pieces to more efficiently use your available storage space.

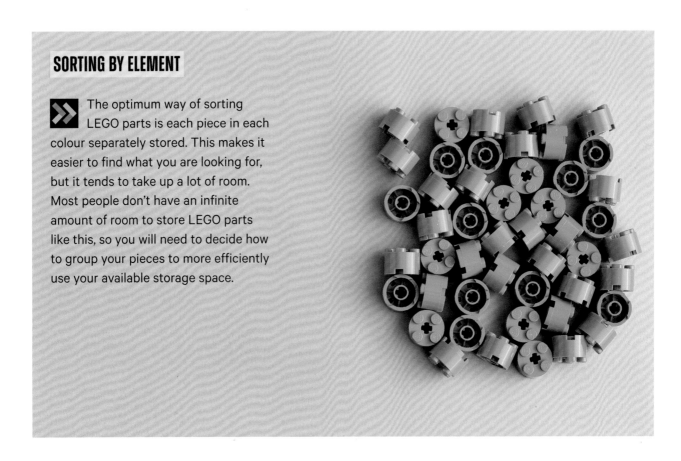

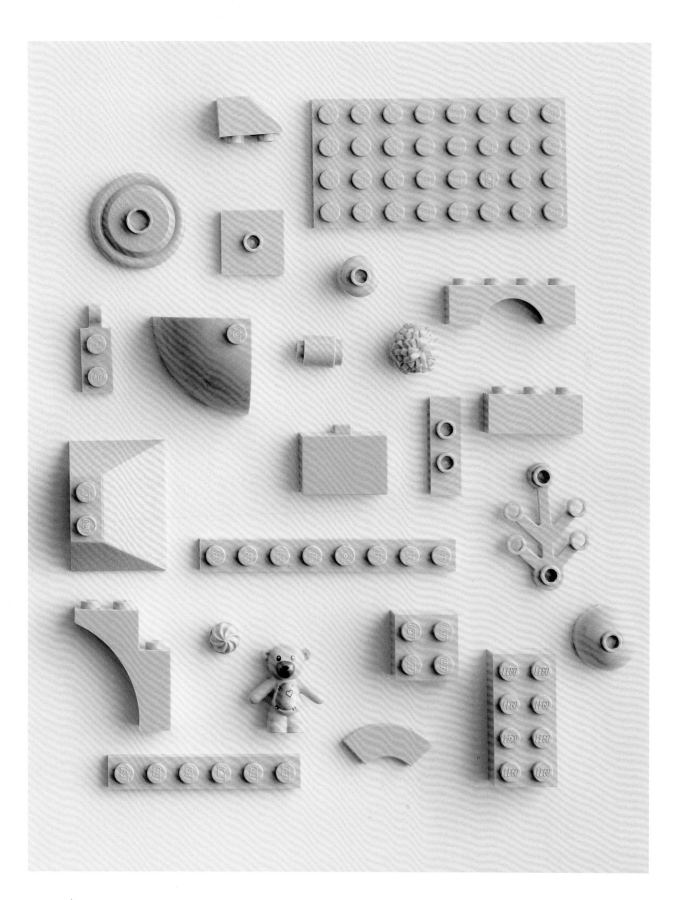

SORTING BY TYPE

Sorting by the type of piece is a little harder, but means you have all of the same type of piece together regardless of colour, in one container. You know where the pieces are, but not necessarily what colours you have in that piece. Although you might not have a piece in the right colour, you will be able to select an alternative colour fairly easily.

SORTING BY SET

Keeping LEGO sets separate from each other is only useful if you wish to build them again at a later point. If you intend to use these pieces to build MOCs, though, this method makes it very hard to find the parts you need. You may have one kind of piece, such as tree tops, spread over several different sets, and you then need to find each one. If you intend building your own models with the pieces from sets, sort them in one of the other ways.

SORTING BY CATEGORY

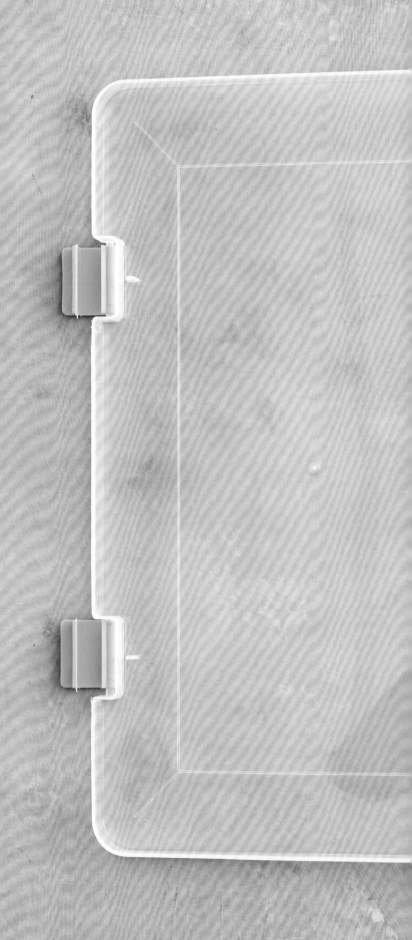

▶▶ Keeping parts that have similar functions together can be beneficial. Think about the different kinds of parts in your collection and what would be useful to store together. Different categories to start you off could be: bricks, plates, tiles, round bricks, slopes, curves, wedges, hinges, connection pieces, SNOT bricks, brackets, hinges, Technic™, animals, plants, baseplates, minifigure parts and accessories, doors and windows, windscreens, wheels, bars, fences, flowers and ladders.

When sorting, be sure to store printed and transparent pieces in small amounts in their own small containers, as storing large numbers of them together and with other pieces will scratch the prints and mark the surface of the transparent pieces. Resealable plastic bags will stop pieces moving about a lot as you can squeeze the air out of the bag so the soft plastic gently holds the parts still.

The more you move your LEGO parts around against each other, the more the surfaces will get scratched, so avoid putting your LEGO collection in large containers that you have to sift through.

LEGO CARE

You don't want to use anything too harsh or rough when cleaning LEGO bricks and pieces. Soft-bristled make-up brushes and sponges are good for cleaning and dusting small detailed areas, paintbrushes of different sizes are good if you need to use a little more elbow grease, and for larger sections a feather duster should do the trick (see *Toolkit*, page 31).

Try to get out of the habit of blowing on your model; instead use other methods to remove little bits of stuff. Blowing on the model can spread germs and may result in adding moisture from your breath. A rubber air-blower bulb – photographers use them for cleaning cameras – is excellent for removing things without having to blow on the model. Blowing may also make you light-headed and if you are prone to dizziness, the air blower is a handy tool.

You can also buy pressurised cans of air to blow dust and dirt particles off your LEGO model. These are available at hobby shops, department stores, hardware stores and some office supplies stores.

A clean microfibre cloth is a great way to get any greasy fingermarks, spots, dirt and other marks off the surface of your LEGO model. You want to lift the dirt without scratching or scuffing the LEGO parts. It will look better bright and shiny than greasy, cloudy and scratchy.

If your model gets wet, it's easy to use paper towel to soak up moisture without leaving threads from fabric or bits of sponge. Tiny shreds of paper can be easily blown away once they are dry. Sections that are very dirty or covered in sticky drink spills can be cleaned with a regular dishwashing detergent and warm water. You may need to dismantle dirty sections to get the bits out from in between pieces. Dry them on butcher's paper, or use tea towels. Shake out any water that has collected in recesses.

Do not use very hot or boiling water on LEGO parts as it can change the structural bonds of the plastic and weaken the parts, making them look cloudy and dull, and may even slightly melt them, deforming them enough to make them unusable.

Do not display your LEGO models in direct sunlight for long periods of time. The UV light and heat can damage the plastic over time, discolouring the pieces and making the plastic brittle. Place your models where they will not be in sunlight and they won't be affected. UV glass tinting can help protect them, but can be expensive.

LEGO LOGISTICS

CLEANING UP AFTERWARDS

Once you've finished building, it's a good idea to clean up after yourself. Sweep the floor and rescue pieces that might need a wash. Sort your leftover LEGO parts and put them back into your sorted storage. Check if pieces that have been on the floor are scratched or otherwise damaged; these will look awful as surface detail, but can still be used as interior structure. If you have a lot of these, start a box of 'filler bricks' that can be used but not seen.

1 X 1 SQUARE GRID TEMPLATE

(available to download at **thebrickman.com/brickman-better-builds-downloads**)

1 X 1.2 VERTICAL GRID TEMPLATE

(available to download at **thebrickman.com/brickman-better-builds-downloads**)

1 X 3.2 TILE EDGE MOSAIC GRID TEMPLATE

(available to download at **thebrickman.com/brickman-better-builds-downloads**)

GLOSSARY

AFOL

Acronym for Adult Fan Of LEGO®. *Usage:* many AFOLs like to use Erling bricks.

ANTI-STUD

The socket in the bottom of a LEGO part that the stud goes into when parts are connected.

BASEPLATE *see also plate*

Baseplates are large flat plates covered in studs but with a smooth underside. They are not essential in a model, but they can help anchor a build and also make it more portable.

BRICK

The basic LEGO building part. Brick sizes in this book are represented by two numbers: the number of studs along the shorter side **x** the number of studs on the longer side – for example, a 1x1-stud brick, a 2x8-stud brick. Bricks are equal to three plates stacked on top of each other.

BRICK-BUILT

A build or part of a build that is made from scratch from LEGO parts, even if a prefabricated version is available.

BUILD

Any LEGO creation; also known as a model.

CHEESE GRATERS, CHEESE SLOPES

The fan name for the sloped LEGO part 'Roof Tile 1x1x2/3' is a cheese slope, so called because in yellow these pieces look like – and have been used in sets as – a wedge of cheese. Cheese graters are similar parts, but the sloped surface consists of a grill or a series of slats.

ERLING BRICK *see also headlight brick, SNOT*

A 1x1-stud brick with a stud on one vertical side. Also known as a washing machine brick or a headlight brick. A Super Erling brick is an Erling brick with studs on all four vertical sides.

FLEX TUBE

A LEGO part that is the same diameter as a standard bar, but is hollow and flexible and comes in some sets in a variety of lengths.

F.L.U.

F.L.U. stands for Fundamental LEGO Unit, and equates to the width and length of a 1x1 LEGO plate or brick. It is useful for calculating LEGO maths (see page 114).

GREEBLE

Small pieces added to the flat surface of a LEGO build to break it up. This makes the model more visually interesting and convincing. Also known as nurnie.

HALF-PIN

A type of LEGO Technic™ pin that is half the length of a regular pin and ends with a hollow LEGO stud.

HEADLIGHT BRICK *see Erling brick, SNOT*

ILLEGAL

Building techniques that are not recommended by the LEGO Group because they may damage the bricks or connectors, such as inserting a plate on its edge between the studs of a brick, are called 'illegal'.

INVENTORY

When you buy an official LEGO set, you will also receive a pictorial list of parts that are included in the box. This is the inventory.

INVERTED PART

This is a LEGO brick, usually specialised in some way (such as part of an arch, or a curved or sloped brick), in which the studs and anti-studs are opposite to the usual placement. For example, a 2x2-stud brick with a 45-degree slope has four anti-studs on the bottom and two studs on top, while the inverted part has four studs on top and two anti-studs on the bottom.

JUMPER PLATE *see also plate*

A plate with the usual configuration of anti-stud sockets on the base but an offset stud on the top; for example, a 1x2-anti-stud plate with only 1 stud in the centre, or a 2x2-anti-stud plate with 1 stud in the centre. These are useful for making steps smaller than a full stud width.

LEGO®

The world's most creative interlocking brick system. Also a children's toy.

LEGOS

This term is wrong, wrong, wrong! LEGO is the brand name, not the name of the part: you build with LEGO bricks, not Legos, and if you want to talk about multiple pieces you can say LEGO parts or LEGO accessories. Incidentally, you always spell LEGO with all capital letters.

LOWELL SPHERE

A 4x4x4-stud sphere constructed using SNOT techniques. The method can be adapted to create tubes and other shapes (see pages 102–105). It was developed by, and named after, Bruce Lowell in 2002.

MECH

A mech or mecha is a large robot or humanoid machine that is operated by a pilot.

MINIFIGURE, MINIFIG

LEGO people were first introduced in 1978 and they have been populating LEGO cities ever since. With interchangeable legs, torsos, arms, heads and hair – plus heaps of cool accessories – you can make all sorts of characters, from aviators to zookeepers.

MIXELS

Mixels™ was a LEGO theme introduced in 2014 and discontinued in 2016, in conjunction with a TV show. Mixels were small creatures who could combine parts with each other, and their elements, such as ball joints and hinges, are very useful parts for creative builds.

MOC

Acronym for My Own Creation. Refers to any fan-made build that is not an official LEGO set. We all love LEGO sets, but sometimes it's fun to create a unique build. *Usage:* 'Your MOCs just keep getting better and better!'

N.P.U.

Nice Part Use. If you use a LEGO part in an unexpected way, you have created an N.P.U.

PART

Any piece made by the LEGO Group. It could be a brick, plate, wheel, axle, minifig hairpiece or flower.

PLATE

A plate is a flat LEGO brick. Three plates stuck together are the same height as a brick. Plates can be many sizes, from 1x1-stud squares and circles to 50x50-stud baseplates.

SNOT *see also headlight brick, stud, tile*

Studs Not On Top. This term can refer to LEGO parts that have smooth surfaces on the top side, such as tiles, or parts that have studs on other surfaces, such as Erling (headlight) bricks or inverted parts. It can also refer to regular parts that are used on their sides or even upside down (see page 126).

STUD

The main interlocking mechanism of LEGO parts is a bump or knob on the top (usually) of a LEGO part that fits inside an anti-stud on the bottom (usually) of another part. You can measure bricks and builds by counting the number of studs.

TECHNIC

LEGO Technic™ is one of the core ranges for older kids and adults, but many of its basic components, such as pins and beams, have become common in a lot of other LEGO sets. Technic has robust connections and makes it easy to add moving parts to a build.

TILE

A plate with a smooth top, useful for creating a smooth surface on a build. Tiles can be square, round or other shapes. Some tiles have stickers that turn them into specific items, such as a stop sign or a pizza.

THE BRICKMAN CHALLENGE ANSWERS

How many Brickman minifigures did you count in the previous pages?

There are 31, plus five impostors.

Did you find the impostors? Usually our Brickman minifigure wears a red top and white pants, except these ones:

Page 56 This tall Brickman has red pants and a white top.
Page 62 Brickman's 'reflection' has his colours the wrong way around.
Page 142 Brickman is dressed as a vampire.
Page 152 Brickman has been scared so much his colours have switched!
Page 268 The duplicate Brickman on the right has red pants, a white top and a red hat.

THANKS

I've never seen myself as an author, so it can only be described as constantly self-shocking that I'm now up to my third book. Of course, making a third book means I've had lots of help from lots of people, so in no particular order:

Darren and Mark, you guys know things about the way LEGO bricks go together that even have me scratching my head.

Everyone at the Brickman team, you make and create LEGO models like nobody else on the planet: your creativity, ingenuity and passion are what makes us the LEGO builders we are today.

Everybody on the Murdoch Books team: Jacqui, Jane, Kristy, Mark, Melody and Virginia. Who knew making cool books was so much fun?

To Helene, Tormod, Troy, Angie and Leah, thank you for all of your support from the LEGO Group.

Thanks also to Mum and Nana, for getting me interested in LEGO bricks all those years ago.

Finally, to D-Mac, AJ, Hamish and everyone involved in the making of *LEGO Masters Australia*. We really do push the question of 'What makes a brilliant LEGO model?' and this book goes some way to answering that. Oh, and of course to everyone who watches *LEGO Masters Australia*, thanks for supporting us and keeping the brick-building going.

RYAN M^cNAUGHT

INDEX

Published in 2022 by Murdoch Books, an imprint of Allen & Unwin

Murdoch Books Australia
Cammeraygal Country
83 Alexander Street
Crows Nest NSW 2065
Phone: +61 (0)2 8425 0100
murdochbooks.com.au
info@murdochbooks.com.au

Murdoch Books UK
Ormond House
26–27 Boswell Street
London WC1N 3JZ
Phone: +44 (0) 20 8785 5995
murdochbooks.co.uk
info@murdochbooks.co.uk

For corporate orders and custom publishing,
contact our business development team
at salesenquiries@murdochbooks.com.au

Publisher: Jane Morrow
Editorial Manager: Virginia Birch
Design Manager: Kristy Allen
Creative Direction and Design: Northwood Green
Editor: Melody Lord
Photographer: Mark Roper
Prop Stylist: Deborah Kaloper, Lee Blaylock
Production Director: Lou Playfair

LEGO, the LEGO logo and the Minifigure
are all trademarks of the LEGO Group.
© 2022 The LEGO Group

*Murdoch Books acknowledges the Traditional
Owners of the Country on which we live and
work. We pay our respects to all Aboriginal and
Torres Strait Islander Elders, past and present.*

ISBN 978 1 92261 627 2 Australia
ISBN 978 1 91166 858 9 UK

A catalogue record for this
book is available from the
National Library of Australia

A catalogue record for this book is available
from the British Library.

Colour reproduction by Splitting Image Colour
Studio Pty Ltd, Clayton, Victoria
Printed by C&C Offset Printing Co. Ltd., China

10 9 8 7 6 5 4 3 2 1

FSC
www.fsc.org
MIX
Paper | Supporting
responsible forestry
FSC® C008047